A HEARTBROKEN DAUGHTER

STEPHEN BRADLEY-WATERS

ISBN: 9798622405242

DEDICATION

For my beautiful daughter.

She has shown courage, perseverance and resilience.

A HEARTBROKEN DAUGHTER

by Stephen Bradley-Waters

NON-FICTION

A Father's Daughter
A Heartbroken Daughter

CONTENTS

AUTHOR'S NOTE

Writing *A Father's Daughter* was liberating. A chance to correct the lies and tell the real story; forever one of my most significant accomplishments.

It weighs heavily on me that what happens after Family Court often goes unsaid. Peoples lives unravel, but rarely a documentation of the struggles or liberation in those proceeding months and years later. *A Heartbroken Daughter* is a continuation of *A Father's Daughter* which documented the Court process, and now what happens after Court proceedings. Writing *A Heartbroken Daughter* has been tormenting with my mind exhausted; often struggling to proceed on numerous occasions. I get no satisfaction from telling such a personal story just a sense of frustration, loss, and bewilderment.

I share my thoughts and feelings on everything that has happened as I see them. The other parties involved may see things differently, but I cannot speak on their behalf. Bitterness and frustrations threatened to derail the story but with time comes wisdom and in-turn reflection.

Casey has put our daughter and me through a living hell. Her decisions ultimately lead to a chaotic life as she places herself before others. While her choices and behaviour are often shocking and disturbing, I do know that Casey loves Jessie very much. Sometimes hate and spite cloud judgement so she continues to hurt me, and in the process, our daughter. As a strange coincidence like *A Father's Daughter* was completed on Father's Day, the writing process of *A Heartbroken Daughter* concluded on Casey's birthday. I finished three months ahead of schedule.

There were moments when I questioned whether to continue writing, stop, move on, and put it all behind me. These moments were frequent. Even as I finished writing the story, the pondering whether to publish was ever-present. It hasn't been an easy process or a decision taken lightly, nor has it been done for malice. Courts make decisions every day, which affect the lives of many. Often those decisions are endured in silence. I felt strongly that for once, in my daughters' case at least, our situation needed to be documented and shared.

PROLOGUE

The events of A Father's Daughter were unexpected and traumatising. My daughter Jessie was abducted from school by her mother. Jessie's half-sister Emma was also taken away with them, but Casey has full residency of her so she was free to do as and what she wants without recompense. It is this power and control which she is used to that governs her reluctance to share any decision making. They had been spending a couple of days at the grandparents home to give Casey, and I time apart. Our relationship had been in decline for many months; however, nothing prepared me for what she would unwittingly decide.

We had agreed during the turmoil before these events that were we to separate then we would split the residency of Jessie evenly. One week with the mother, and the other with me. We expected each other to live locally. Jessie had chosen to live with me but was open to a shared residence to maintain relationships with her mother and half-sister. There was no indication that anyone was unhappy with this arrangement until the weekend before the incident.

Casey and I had had a terrible day together. We were arguing and spouting negative remarks at each other. It was a day from hell, the worst in our entire relationship. Probably more so because we were growing apart and losing the love we once shared. As the days built up, we resented each other. Her more than me, but inside I required a change, even if I could not admit it to myself. She had been going away weekends for the past couple of months, making no effort to call the kids. Jessie would stay in my care. Emma with the grandparents, which I never understood. Casey surprised me by declaring that she would now be applying for full custody of Jessie. It made little sense as we still reside together, so what would be the point? And we both knew the mental health issues she contended with daily with the responsibility placed continuously upon me. I was the stable parent; supporting Casey through her problems while being a mainstay in the children's lives, making sure that they are unaffected by her behaviour.

On Monday just a few short days before Jessie's seventh birthday our lives changed forever. I had expected to speak with her on the phone before she returns home the next day. Phone calls went unanswered. I was not aware at that moment that Casey had blocked my phone number. A plan which she had been arranging was now in full effect — all of which behind my back. I was bewildered and felt helpless. My daughter and I ripped apart. I contacted the police to check on her welfare as I felt dread and despair when I realised what had happened. The full custody comment just a few days prior now tormented my mind. If only I had

8

noticed the signs. Maybe I could have prevented it from happening — a regret of mine which I have to endure.

Today I know what happened. At the time, I could only follow intuition and advice: piece together everything like a detective. Complete the puzzle, no matter how confusing and heartbreaking. Jessie needed me to be at my best and fight to overturn this injustice to her life. Time was of the essence.

Eighteen months prior, Casey found herself sectioned at a mental health ward of a hospital. I supported her each day, never missing a visitation. In her words, I was her rock. I have all of the messages between us on record. Her mother had done plenty of research on what is required to get Casey released. It is this manipulation and extensive research, which has me believe that her mother wanted to use abuse against me. It gets Casey what she wants, and quickly. In-fact shortly after she had left the hospital, her mother wanted Casey to apply for social housing without me. She tried to use abuse to speed the application; however, Casey refused to accuse me of such a slanderous claim.

Casey fled to a local refuge in April 2017 which had been pre-planned earlier in February during a secret meeting with her mother and a mental health worker. A strategic claim of abuse made against me. Strangely around this time, Casey had sent me a text asking whether I would accompany her for a weekend spa retreat.

I was lost and anxious so messaged Casey's family and friends trying to get in contact and find out what is happening. Everyone ignored all of my requests. I tried visiting the home of her parents, but there was no response. These attempts to get in touch with Casey gave her the excuse she needed to change refuge and get away from this supposed abusive ex-partner.

They had only stayed locally for a couple of days, then swiftly relocated to Liverpool. Connor, this new friend of Casey's, met them on the train as they approached the city. He greeted the children, telling them not to worry as he is a friend of their mothers. Connor would become more than that as time went on, and I believe he was more than that when she had decided to leave me, let alone arrive in his hometown. A perfectly orchestrated new life. It would explain her weekends away and not calling the children as she was on her love trysts behind my back. More sickening is that we had gone shopping during the week. Casey had bought new matching underwear. Would turn out to be for Connors benefit while purchasing with me by her side. More fool me, I guess. She knew what she was doing. It just shows her narcissistic mindset.

I urgently acquired a solicitor to support me through the legal obstacles in pursuit of getting Jessie home. They were incredibly supportive and so enamoured with my case that they had a meeting and made a decision to take on my case pro-bono. They would not charge me anything for their services. Witnessing such generosity for my daughter bought me to tears. They could see how much Jessie means to me. The moment that topped it off was when I made an offer to Casey. If she brings Jessie back and keeps her in the same school, she has always attended and adheres to our original agreement of shared residency; I would give her my home. They were my only terms. Casey never did respond. I honestly thought at that time that she had done this solely for our shared home. Little did I know that she had found a new love interest and changed everyone's lives to be near him.

For a while, the kids did not attend a school which was one of my concerns. I knew that there was a risk of disruption to their lives which would harm their education and mental wellbeing. After all the abrupt changes to their lives; moving away from family and friends and living in unfamiliar surroundings were bound to be unsettling.

Jessie broke down in tears when she realised that she would not be returning to the family home. Casey and her mother witnessed her inconsolable, yet she was the least of their concerns. Emma has always been the family favourite on Casey's side. I am sure that she was complicit in what happened as it transpires that she was manipulating Casey during our time living together — telling her lies about me to instigate us arguing. Casey used to fly into a rage for no apparent reason. Now I know why - Emma.

Casey continued to play the victim to everyone she met from family and friends to healthcare and legal professionals. Engaging in communication was agonisingly slow. She had no interest in talking and working out the situation. For her, there was no negotiating. Her stance changed when she realised that I would not relent on pursuing her through solicitors. She finally acquired a solicitor of her own after a couple of months of being ignorant. Even then, she was never enthusiastic about her responses.

Casey's solicitors sent a letter. The contents were deplorable. The accusation was that I had emotionally abused Casey and Emma while using Jessie as a means to control them. It was absurd. I had a feeling that it would come to this. It was not unexpected but hurt all the same. While waiting for Casey to engage for the past couple of months, I had been piecing everything together. After following all of the dots, it had become evident that there would be an accusation of abuse. A few years ago, the law changed regarding applications for Legal Aid in the UK. Financial destitution was no longer enough to be granted; awarded only to victims of abuse. It did not take a rocket scientist to predict what she would be saying about me. It was made clear that I am to have no further involvement in Emma's life, which hurt me more than anyone would know. Casey had told me before that Emma would be allowed to stay over with me were we to live apart, so that was unexpected. She had also mentioned a family meal once a month for the sake of the kids. Now all of a sudden, I am so evil that she wants nothing more to do with me. Yet just over a year prior I was her saviour during the lowest moments of her life. In fact I was still supporting her well into the new year; how times change. I filed a Child's Arrangements Order application with the Family Court in Liverpool immediately.

I had found Casey's parents home phone number a month or so prior. My mum phoned to try and mediate between parties. Her mum responded with abusive language and accused me of abuse; stating that I need to get my head checked. A reference to me being crazy. Mum in response, said like-wise about Casey. It got heated. I did say to mum that I hope she did not say negatives about Casey as I do not want that. At that time, I still felt protective of her and thought that she was under the narcissistic spell of her mother. Mum was fuming about the mother. More so than I had realised at the time. My step-dad asked me to intervene and calm her down. I encouraged her to handle this the right way through the courts.

The first court hearing was only a preliminary. Casey tried to manipulate me into abdicating my legal responsibility of Jessie, using our desire to see each other as a way to get one hand closer to full-residency of her. I did not give it a moments thought as I declined immediately. The time between the next hearing was chaotic and in all honesty, disgusting. Jessie had been upset about missing home. So much so that she had told her teachers at school who intervened and spoke to Casey. She did her usual nodding positively, however, unbeknown to them she would not take any of it into consideration. The Court had ordered her to encourage Jessie and help her write letters to me fortnightly. I was to do the same in return. I sent letters and attached magazines for Jessie. I never once received a message during this period.

Casey responded through solicitors stating that she only said she would try to encourage her, not force her, and that they had been too busy with school runs which were absurd.

13

Nothing changed in the school summer holidays — no efforts to facilitate a conversation between Jessie and me. Meanwhile, Emma was having phone calls with her dad and visiting our hometown to spend time with their side of the family. Jessie had to endure losing the people she loved with no form of communication. She was locked away like the step-sister in Cinderella.

Throughout Court proceedings, it was chaotic. Casey used every opportunity to disrupt and hinder my contact with Jessie. She would act scared of me to play on her victim status. There were many highs and lows, all of which affected Jessie deeply. Casey never once thought of how her decisions impacted on Jessie. Her sole aim was to obstruct and prevent. The longer Court took to conclude the harder it would be to get Jessie home.

We had many contacts together, starting with a few hours, which increased over time to Jessie coming home for holidays and weekends. On a couple of occasions, Casey lied to the Judge which temporarily suspended our contact. She miraculously changed her stance on both occasions when I contested the decision at the next Court hearing. To my surprise, the Judge praised her, rather than reprimand her for wasting time and emotionally harming our daughter.

It was the tip of the iceberg. I was only ever there in Court for Jessie. Casey was there for herself, evident by all of her demands and restrictions of access she requested. I never relented as I fought fire with fire. I never made it easy on her, and a few times, I came close to getting Jessie home. In the end, the final decision was incredibly close. It could've

14

gone either way. The Judge was visibly in favour of Jessie returning to me. He questioned the appointed CAFCASS Guardian on her reasoning as he suspected that her decisions favoured Emma rather than what is best for Jessie. I suspect now after much reflection that she chose to keep the status quo to maintain the relationships in Jessie's life. I had shown myself capable and determined to travel to spend time with Jessie against all of the difficulties and costs. If Jessie returned to me, then she could lose her mother and sister as they are reluctant to travel. It isn't fair that I must carry the burden of travelling and neither Jessie or I getting the life we desire simply because of her mother. I believe that was the overriding factor.

After questioning from my barrister and persistence from the Judge, the Guardian had no choice but to admit that Casey had emotionally harmed Jessie in abducting her and relocating so far away from friends and family. She never once said anything negative about me. After many of the Court hearings, my barrister often said that the Judge had much respect for me. In his summing up he also made a statement: No-one can be left in any doubt the love that exists between Jessie and her father and vice-versa. It's clear to me that the father's application to the Court was made for the sole purpose of his daughter.

Jessie had consistently stated her desire to return home. She even wrote a letter to the Judge pleading to let her come back to daddy. I was in tears at the thought of Jessie losing the hope she had clung to for so long upon hearing the final decision. It wasn't the outcome either of us wished for.

'Children begin by loving their parents; after a time they judge them; rarely, if ever, do they forgive them.'

- Oscar Wilde

A HEARTBROKEN DAUGHTER

1

DESIRES

My daughter Jessie continues to grow and mature since being ordered by the Court to reside with her mother. A decision, both of us struggle to comprehend. She is now ten-years-old. Her desires never change, wanting to live back at home with me - her father. For now, we suffer injustice.

I sacrifice to keep our relationship alive. Pass up excellent career opportunities to make myself available. Travel the excruciating distance alternate weekends; one thousand miles. Back and forth Friday, and the same for her return Sunday. Sadly Jessie has to endure five hundred miles of the journey. Not fair for any child. She would, however, not have it any other way.

Our time together is too precious. I often think I'm doing everything for her. She deserves no less. The reality is that I am also doing it for me. I couldn't bear living a life without her. My heart would be empty and any success meaningless. Almost a year on from the final Court hearing a rare opening came my way at a local airport. An incredible opportunity, one I struggled to dismiss. I knew it would be damaging for Jessie with our time together already limited. The desire I have for the perfect life, well the best it could be, for now, tormented me.

Initially, I decided not to pursue the job and missed the induction. The weight of disappointment, however, consumed me. I hastily rearranged the initiation and paid for a basic criminal record check which is a requirement for an air-side pass. It came back all clear. In my mind, I could make the job work even with a strange rota and hours: evenings and nights, six days on three off. Working out the weekend contact was a nightmare. No matter how much I wanted it to be okay, It wasn't. I knew after accepting the job; I had broken Jessie's heart. I can't begin to explain how sad that made me feel.

I never wanted her to suffer turmoil from my actions. Her mother's caused enough chaos for a lifetime. I was trying to make the best of the situation. Sadly she continues to dictate my life. After much consideration, I didn't attend the induction and informed the manager of my decision. He graciously understood.

A desire lingers within me to be successful and make Jessie proud. I won't, however, allow that to be a burden that hurts her. She always comes first and will continue to do so. No one's life is truly perfect. There will be disappointments and failures. Jessie will always be the light that shines the brightest in my life. If it's a choice of being successful and having a fantastic career with wealth and prosperity or being by Jessie's side as she grows, then she wins every time. Love and sincerity are priceless. I stand by her side whenever she needs me.

I found it strange and alarming that the people involved with child welfare stop their involvement immediately after Court proceedings. It took me off-guard. Surely the Court would like to seek assurances that the transition goes smoothly. Monitoring a child during the immediate aftermath of a decision should be the least of their responsibilities. After the Court's decision, a letter arrived from CAFCASS informing that the case-worker had been re-assigned.

There was no further point of contact; complaining to solicitors got nowhere. They expected life to become functional with time and patience - an incredible naivety in the entire process from everyone. Expecting disruptive parties to drop their egos and behave responsibly when they can wield power is surreal. Who makes up these laws? Courts frown upon parents returning within a few years of a decision, so hands are tied in that regard. Who is there to turn too? I didn't know, and I still don't know. I can only direct Jessie to her school teachers and hope that they act if she is traumatised. On my end, I can only document and be ready to fight again when the doors open, and the Court allows. The system is flawed on so many levels. Time and time again, children are left to suffer in silence.

It's been a challenging year, in the same way, the preceding years were chaotic. The circumstances haven't changed just the rules we abide. Casey continues to be unpredictable. Pleasant one minute then the devil incarnate the next. One would think that having a new house and residency of Jessie she would be happy. That is certainly not the case, and I can't help but wonder whether she regrets any of her actions. Time was always going to be the final judge on everything that has happened. Slowly the truth unravels.

2

REVELATION

Casey took it upon herself to inform Jessie of the Court's decision. She made it clear that she wished to tell Jessie delicately, in a way only a mother could. If Casey was sincere, then I had no problem with the arrangement.

Plans were in place for Jessie and me to spend a couple of hours together after school the following day. We would meet at a McDonald's in a location alien to me. An area I had never visited, but apparently, she would find familiar. She arrived with the broadest smile. Our eyes locked and didn't distract. Connor tried to make himself the centre of attention by making a fuss of Jessie as she attempted to walk the last few yards into my care. It was futile as her attention wasn't on him. It was on me. No matter how hard he tries to force her love, I will always be her father, and there is nothing more substantial than the love between a father and daughter.

As always, Jessie likes to jump all over me and be rather silly, which is something we both enjoy. The conversation soon turned to the courts' decision.

"Did mummy tell you about court?" I asked.

"Yeah."

"Are you okay?"

"Yeah," Jessie said with an air of uncertainty. Her body language told a different story of sadness and disappointment.

"How did she tell you?"

"On the bus home."

"On the bus?" I asked. Immediately agitated that a critical conversation involving Jessie's life was informed so casually.

"Yep."

"Did you like that she told you on the bus?"

"No. Mum doesn't like me bothering her so I couldn't ask anything. She said it like it wasn't a big deal."

The situation had me at boiling point. Not only have Jessie and I faced an incredible injustice, but Casey dared to take it upon herself to inform Jessie of a life-changing decision on a *bus*. Either it was done in this way on purpose so that Jessie doesn't cause a scene or Casey didn't deem it significant. Either way, she has shown herself to be incompetent and not able to relate to children.

During Court proceedings, I had requested to collect Jessie from school, which the judge approved. I asked Jessie if she would like to show me her school so that I know where I'm going when it's time to get her. She was eager to show me, so we left McDonald's and drove the short journey. A small car park adorned the path to the school behind a petrol garage. My sister Shelly was present, though she decided to wait in the car. Jessie and I went for a stroll up the path to take a closer look. She pointed and explained where she comes out and lines up at the end of the day. I absorbed everything she told me as I was eager to collect her without any issues.

Like most schools, there was a nearby park. A long single path led to a playground area with a large field to the left, with trees and bushes to the right—an accessible location for dog walkers.

As we were walking, Jessie had plenty on her mind.

"Connor's moved into our house."

"What? Are you sure he's moved in?"

"Yeah, he's been bringing his things around and sleeping over."

"Unbelievable. If you get any problems, let me know."

"Okay. I will."

Throughout Court proceedings, I had made the Court aware that Casey is in a relationship. She continually denied, stating that she was single, meanwhile Connor moved in the same day Court concluded. I had raised the issue for two reasons:

1. Casey isn't capable of caring for the children on her own.

2. Casey is in a relationship from day one, confirming the real reason she relocated so abruptly.

"Mum's engaged. They got engaged during the summer holidays." Jessie said casually.

I was gob-smacked, not through jealousy. I don't care what Casey does with her life. I was disgusted that she had sat in a Court of law denying any relationships as though I had an agenda while in the knowledge that she is engaged. It blows my mind. I shouldn't be surprised by her calculated responses, but this was a step further than even I expected. Wow.

As the conversation developed, it became increasingly apparent that Jessie's half-sister Emma and Connor despise each other. Emma more so, but, Connor never seems to get on with her. I didn't want Jessie to dwell on recent events. Lord knows she could do with a break from the mayhem. Jessie played in the park, and we had some fun with hide-and-seek. She wanted to show me some horses but, they weren't visible from where she had previously seen them. Jessie was despondent, as she had been excited to share the experience. To make her smile, I tried to climb a tree, failing with each attempt much to Jessie and Shelly's amusement. Jessie then tried, but she failed too, which was funny to witness.

I was aware that time was fading. We didn't get much time together as it was just a convenience contact. As I had been up north throughout Court during the week, a short visit was agreed for us to spend a few hours together.

"Connor's mum's house is near here." Jessie remarked.

"Their house is right by your school?"

"Yeah."

"How could no-one have noticed that throughout Court? When people were doing their checks, they should have known. Bloody hell."

"He went to my school when he was a kid."

26

"That would explain why you have to get up so early and travel so far for school."

"Mum's at their house now."

"She went back there after dropping you off?"

"Yeah. Mum's taking me back there after."

"Makes no sense to travel back to McDonald's, for you to then come back when you're already here."

I then sent Casey a text message explaining where we are and the convenience of collecting her from the park. For her to be just a few roads away was surreal.

"I don't want to go back." Jessie said as she clung to me.

"I know. We have no choice at the moment." I explained.

"Emma's always horrible and rude to me. Mum doesn't care." She said as she looked down at the ground.

It broke my heart to witness my daughter so sad. We only find ourselves in this situation because everyone else lied. Emma sent an endearing letter to the Court detailing the love she has for Jessie and the profound loss she would feel if she weren't with her. The reality is so much different. Casey herself can't seem to differentiate between truth and lies. Her imagination runs wild, believing any thought that comes into her head. To her, she's the victim. Everyone should feel sorry for *her*, but the reality is that she is a heartless narcissist. She should be ashamed of herself.

Casey arrived shortly after receiving the text message. Connor appeared by her side, looking full of himself. The impression I had of him wasn't of an upgrade. A messy, overgrown beard, bland hairstyle and odd attire left me confused about the appeal. I would later ask Shelly "What am I missing?", she couldn't figure it out either. Jessie had told me that that he is somewhat controlling, can be fun at times but that's rare. His anger frightens her. Not the catch I had expected and hardly enhancing the children's lives.

Emma and I had our battles throughout the years as she is stubborn, selfish and arrogant. I tried in vain to warm her personality, but it just caused friction between us. It appears that Connor has the same issues I contended. The difference is that I loved her and just wanted to help her develop into a well-rounded individual. He, on the other hand, hates her. I know this from everything Jessie has told me. Whenever they talk, it always ends in arguments. Neither of them has embraced the word "Sorry".

I never give Connor any of my attention during hand-overs. I'm only there for one reason - Jessie. He can look all he likes; it's obvious he craves attention. That's something he will never get from me. Casey may have caused everything that has happened, but to me, he is a manipulative home wrecker. Whether he is charming in between the angry moments is inconsequential. It doesn't make up for the distress caused to Jessie's life.

3

MUM

I'm not a religious man, but I am open to spiritual possibilities. Maybe that ties into religion, I'm not quite sure. Just simply open-minded. I don't go around preaching or pushing my thoughts onto others. My views and opinions are my own, and I respect others for their beliefs. I've experienced enough to know that there's a big possibility that there is more beyond what we can see and feel. For instance, rodents can hear higher frequencies than humans. Does that mean that because we can't hear it, then it doesn't exist? No, of course not. The same should then apply for other forms of anomalies.

The encounters that I have had, often raised the hairs on my body to stand on edge. Cold energy passed through in a room with no breeze. Apparitions appeared in photos and videos, noises and psychic readings validate my experiences, for me. All of this long-winded explanation to say that mum is my guardian angel. The epitome of what a parent should aspire to be, nurturing, supportive and selfless. Don't get me wrong we are both incredibly similar, good and bad. We don't put up with nonsense and quick to stand up for ourselves. Heated arguments can happen, rarely, but it happens. She is the worst to engage, as she doesn't listen and repeats the same ramblings as fact. Annoying beyond belief.

Then there is the side to her that everyone would dream of having; a mother that has supported me for my entire life — by my side throughout all of the good and bad. In-fact she was the first person to hold my daughter, even before Casey or me. I was worried about Casey after such an exhausting delivery, and she was in no state to comprehend what had happened, let alone hold a baby. Mum's hands were the first to embrace the precious life that is my daughter Jessie.

When moments get too hard, and I begin to self-doubt, she is there to keep me going. I'm incredibly strong-willed, always have been. I think it comes from knowing that she is there by my side. Never alone or fighting solo. She is my wings when I need to fly. Without her, maybe I wouldn't be so strong. Perhaps I wouldn't be the me that I love. I like who I am — a mirror image of my mother.

I travel the earth for Jessie. It's not easy, the journey is long and demoralising, at least for those return moments. Mind exhausted, eyes strained, body aching - especially knees. Arduous but Jessie is worth the suffering. To make myself available for her, I've had to turn down some great career opportunities. Offers that I can't afford to dismiss. It's gut-wrenching having to weigh up and decide everything with pros and cons. In the end, Jessie always outweighs everything. The issue is I need the income to travel and of course pay the bills, but if the time isn't available to see Jessie, then what's the point of money. A regular conflict in my mind.

My mum is the saviour. While I do all the travel and throw my body on the line time and time again, she supports my cause; financially assisting until I am able. Without her, my commitment and sacrifice would be in vain. It would be impossible to travel further than out of town, let alone the breadth of the country and back. For this, I will be eternally grateful, and I am sure I can speak for Jessie too.

Mum hates me travelling alone. I don't know why because I enjoy the open road, and singing along to music. Having company is helpful but not entirely necessary. She works as a nurse at a nearby hospital. Before that, she worked at a nursing home. She is always helping people and popular with colleagues and patients. Mum is friendly with many friends and visitors. I get that side from her, but I can be the polar opposite at times, reclusive and isolated. I have it in me to be either way and comfortable. The best part of me though is the outgoing, sociable and funny character that people enjoy. Mum also has that in abundance. She prefers the company of others while I try to break free now and then.

When she has a free day coinciding with my travels, she makes herself available. An entire day lost to travel. She likes the company and being near Jessie, but I think she's motivated to make sure we are safe. She sacrifices for me as I do Jessie. I appreciate any admiration that I receive;

however, my mum deserves it more. Without her, none of this would be possible.

4

COUNSELLOR

To my surprise, Jessie was receiving counselling sessions during school. There was no mention of this within any Court order or statements. Casey had never said anything to me about this arrangement. The situation is exasperating. From my understanding, the sessions are with someone from Casey's support system. Possibly Women's Aid, I think Jessie said 'Helping Hands'. It meant nothing to me as I didn't know the reason for the sessions or the expected outcome. Was it a tactic to try and cause more chaos? Who knows.

"Why do you have to talk to someone during school?" I asked.

"Mummy said it's to do with my anger issues."

My blood pressure increased at the thought of Jessie hearing she has anger issues. She is the most pleasant, fun, caring and charismatic person I have ever met. She amazes me in every way. Casey can't handle having a conversation with Jessie about the situation she finds herself. She then palms her off onto someone else to have a *chat*. It's ridiculous and making Jessie feel insecure. She's questioning herself and whether she is a good girl. What kind of parent does that to their child? The torment and anguish on Jessie's face were heartbreaking.

"You are the happiest and funniest child I've ever met. Don't let Mummy make you feel any different," I said.

"Mummy said I have issues."

"Mummy's a lunatic. Never let anyone make you feel bad about yourself. Mummy, me or anyone. Okay,"

"Okay."

"I'm serious. If anyone thinks your angry, then they need their heads checked."

To that, Jessie laughed. My praise reassured her. With me, she never receives negatives about herself. Why would she? Casey brings her down to try and get her down to her depressed level.

Jessie and I had a short writing session during our time together. She was impressed with my poems. I then suggested I could probably write a song if I tried hard enough, as they mostly resemble rhyming poems. To Jessie's astonishment, I had written the song. She liked it. I did do a couple of audio recordings, but my vocals are on the rather lousy end of the spectrum. A printed copy was given to Jessie to keep.

When Casey found out about my song, she was outraged. The ever predictable reaction to anything that resembles the truth. She hates me talking openly about everything that's happened. I'm sure *A Father's Daughter* got a reaction of mega proportions though she's never spoken to me about it, and I wouldn't expect her to read the book.

Casey felt so strongly about the song being in bad taste that she bought it to the attention of Jessie's counsellor. When the counsellor was alone with Jessie, it became clear that she liked the song. Praising my efforts and saying it's rather good. Jessie was thrilled and proud of me. Yet again Casey has shown herself up, over-reacting to anything. She shot herself in the foot again; the counsellor told Jessie that she doesn't think she's an angry child. In-fact Jessie is rather happy and chirpy — the opposite of what Casey had been portraying. By the end of Court the judge, solicitors and barristers could see through Casey, and now an appointed counsellor she had requested could see through her too.

The positive is that Jessie had grown a bond with her and enjoyed their sessions together. She explained that she gets to miss some lessons and have fun with Julie. A silver lining and thankfully not as traumatic as it could've been.

Jessie was sad and rather upset when Julie informed her that the session would be their last. They had had a good few sessions each week, becoming part of Jessie's school routine. When I had initially heard of the counsellor, I wasn't best pleased and outraged. Witnessing Jessie's fondness of the sessions and blossoming friendship made me realise how isolated she is up North with her mother. Having an impartial person to speak openly about her life was great for them both. Jessie could open up without the worry of upsetting anyone and Julie could get a real insight into her life. What her end goal and evaluation is I have no idea, but at the end of the day, I'm not concerned.

The one person she has to confide in when I am not there is her mother. The same person that openly criticises her and lowers her self-esteem. This is the person she must tell her innermost feelings. I hate my daughter having to hold in her feelings, but worse than that is opening your heart to have it crushed and every word twisted against you. That is Casey!

5

POEM SONG

FATHER & DAUGHTER
By Stephen Bradley-Waters

It's never too late to do the right thing,
So much has happened, where to begin?
My mind confused for far too long,
So here it goes in this song.

Some days are good, some days are sad,
    Without my daughter, I'd go mad,
    Whilst we have a sad history, our future is a mystery.
    With my mind up in the clouds,
    Every day, I wake up proud.

    As my daughter sits in class,
    Her mind wanders about our past.
    We joke, we laugh, do silly things,
    Pretend to gallop, cast our wands, fly in the sky with our
wings.

Some days are good, some days are sad,
  Without my daughter, I'd go mad,
  Whilst we have a sad history, our future is a mystery.
  With my mind up in the clouds,
  Every day, I wake up proud.

  Adventures are vast,
  And not our last,
  We travel the country to be close,
  Reduce the distance, between us both.
  We make it south, then back up north,
  Our lives are constantly back and forth.

  Some days are good, some days are sad,
  Without my daughter, I'd go mad,
  Whilst we have a sad history, our future is a mystery.
  With my mind up in the clouds,
  Every day, I wake up proud.

  I sit at home thinking of my little girl,
  I know that she can always tell,
  I mutter a few simple words, "I love you beautiful, please
be happy."
  My little girl always comes first,
  I don't care if I come off worse.

A HEARTBROKEN DAUGHTER

Some see me a villain,
A meanie and abusive,
My only response is simple,
I've done no wrong, and not intrusive,
The only actions are to take care of my daughter,
I don't treat her like I bought her.
She's my world, and the best part of me,
Anyone in their right mind can see...

Some days are good, some days are sad,
Without my daughter, I'd go mad,
Whilst we have a sad history, our future is a mystery.
With my mind up in the clouds,
Every day, I wake up proud.

Tomorrow is a blessing or a curse,
I just hope it doesn't get worse,
Life moves on with our destiny,
My daughter will always get the best of me.

She brightens up every room,
There's no time for doom and gloom.
It's never too late to the right thing,
So much has happened, where to begin?

6

EMMA'S BIRTHDAY

Jessie had the opportunity to join Casey's side of the family to celebrate Emma's birthday in our hometown during the half-term summer holiday. I jumped at the chance. Jessie was excited. While she favours my family and has a more profound connection, she still likes to feel part of the mother's family. Her auntie Becky is a regular source of excitement.

At first, the celebration would take place at Creams. A dessert dinner, specialising in waffles, ice cream and pancakes (crepes). A great place for kids to get a sugar enthused boost. I relayed Jessie's excitement to Casey. Shortly later, the plans altered. Now they may be going to Nandos. Jessie immediately transformed from excitement to apprehension. She can't tolerate spicy food and very particular about her meals. Casey and Emma both knew this. I respected that it's to celebrate Emma's birthday. It's not about Jessie but to change plans upon learning of her enthusiasm caused a fire to burn inside of me. I wasn't impressed.

"They may be going Nandos instead."

"What. I don't know if I will like that."

"The food is spicy, but you like chicken and chips. I'm sure they will do dessert after."

"I don't think I'll like it. Was looking forward to Creams."

"I know, but it's Emma's birthday. Can't be demanding where she celebrates." I explained looking at my despondent daughter with an assuring glance. "Are you comfortable with that?"

"No. I don't want to ruin Emma's birthday if I don't like it." Jessie explained with disappointment echoing from her voice. Her face looked sullenly at the floor.

"I'll explain to mummy. See what she says."

I explained the situation to Casey. She was surprisingly understanding and had a better grasp of the restaurant than me. She explained to Jessie some of the food options she would like, comparing it to dishes served at home. Thankfully Jessie's mood was lifted, and no longer worried.

"Feeling better?"

"Yeah."

So the plans changed again. I can't help but think that someone is messing with Jessie. Either Emma or whoever is planning were undecided, or they were reacting to anything Jessie enjoyed. Playing with her emotions was pushing me over the edge. I was considering putting a stop to it altogether and take her myself to a place she enjoys. For now, I kept my opinion to myself. Biding my time, see how the situation evolves.

We received a final decision just a few hours before Jessie was due to be collected. They would be going to Tangs. A perfect option for everyone. An oriental buffet which serves some English and Italian dishes alongside the Chinese, Thai food and various dessert options. Kids and parents alike enjoy eating there regularly. Jessie was overjoyed, and I was relieved.

Becky collected Jessie from my mothers home. We had spent a few hours there in readiness for her evening excursion. We had waited in the car on the driveway when the time drew nearer for a better view, and I could leave quickly to get home. I cuddled Jessie when Becky came into view after exiting her partner's car. Jessie walked the short distance with confidence. She was waiving back to me as I waved at her. I then drove home, leaving Jessie in her aunties care for the evening.

Upon returning home, Jessie was full of stories. Some fun, others traumatic. She had enjoyed spending time with her aunties and partners. Emma and Jessie had enjoyed some food offerings. The grandmother was the cause of her suffering. Obnoxious, arrogant and malicious. Shouldn't be allowed near children, at the very least Jessie. If I had my way, she would never be allowed near her again. I already had a dislike for her; now there is just revulsion.

She had arrived arguing with the grandfather—swearing in the company of the children. Like Casey, she doesn't seem to have a filter or able to put aside any issues while with the children. Lovely birthday for Emma. Such a charming lady. She even ordered Emma to move to a different seat as she wanted to sit where she was. Her arrogance has no bounds. The part that had me exploding with anger was Jessie explaining that she wanted to join them at the beach after. Instead, ordered to return to me. She wasn't welcome to join them. The words came from the grandmother.

"Can I come with you?"

"NO, YOU CAN NOT!"

An abrupt and arrogant dismissal. At this point, it's unclear who else is aware of her behaviour towards Jessie and whether Casey knows anything. I find it hard to believe that she wouldn't have noticed as it has been going on for years. It stems from a jealousy that Jessie favours me and made her wishes clear that she wants to come home to live. I would like to think that Casey would stand up for Jessie if she did know, but I know she wouldn't. Casey doesn't like confrontation. Could she stand up for Jessie? Unlikely but she does have her moments.

"I'm going to message mummy now. I can't be putting up with this."

"No, please don't, she will get angry."

My heart was torn. This was an issue worth addressing, but Jessie's life up North is delicate, and I'm not there to protect and stand up for her. Against my better judgement, I kept my mouth shut but advised Jessie to have the conversation with her mother as she needs to know. I know Jessie didn't want Casey and I arguing. It escalates so fast like a bush fire. Once we enrage, it gets messy. I didn't want that for Jessie, so I just hoped that she would open up about what happened. To this day, I don't know if she has raised it with her mother. It may be a conversation we need to revisit. For now, I wait to see how the next interaction goes.

7

CHICKEN POX

One of the moments to dread for every child and parent is chickenpox. It started during the Easter holidays. Jessie had a slight fever that gradually worsened. She was becoming increasingly lethargic with each passing day. The symptoms were typical of the common cold and flu. Out of nowhere, she came to me mentioning a spot on her skin. Without initially looking I immediately downplayed it as spots can occur as we grow. It's expected and not a concern. Upon closer inspection, I was aware that it could be a medical issue, but nothing too severe as she had a few scattered sporadically on her body. They appeared to have a small blistered top. Searching Google online narrowed her condition as likely to be chickenpox. Most people contract them at some point in their lifetime so I wasn't too concerned as apparently its safer to get around her age. It's not like we live in a third-world country with no medicine.

I telephoned my mum and sister Shelly to gauge their thoughts and recommendation. Shelly's son Harvey had recently battled Chicken Pox, so I wanted to find out more and share symptoms to garner the severity of the condition. It was only early-onset, so no reason to get anxious and ahead of ourselves. After a little discussion, it was clear that Jessie did in-fact have Chicken Pox.

The next step was to seek medical advice from professionals. I tried my doctors, but they couldn't fit Jessie in with an appointment, which was especially tricky without being registered at my surgery. Casey had registered her elsewhere when she relocated north. All was not lost though, as in the UK we have a 111 telephone service which is an efficient diagnosis system. They take notes over the telephone and provide their advice. If a situation warrants it, then they can refer to the doctor or hospital. Most of the time, a doctor will call back within a few hours of the telephone call ending to follow up.

I had calmed Jessie and explained the possible prognosis. Hearing those words worried her. She was feeling uneasy and concerned. I reassured that she will be okay and that it's best to get it now than when she's older. She could see that I wasn't stressed or anxious. I was in complete control doing my best just to get confirmation and a course of treatment.

The telephone call was straightforward.

"Hi, this is 111 medical service."

"My daughter has got spots appearing on her skin. I think it might be Chicken Pox."

"What makes you think that?"

"I browsed the NHS website and checked the symptoms, which were a match."

"That's the same thing we use to check, so you were right to look there."

"If we go through some checks, we can make sure to find out if it is."

"Okay, that's fine."

They proceeded to ask for my address and then Jessie's. Up until now, I hadn't known Casey's address and never really cared to know either. My credit report happened to have a shared debt registered at a previous address she resided. Probably the refuge she was staying. Again it was of no interest to me. Casey likes to play the victim, but I have no interest in where she is. On this occasion, it was urgent. They asked me of an address in Liverpool which I asked Jessie to verify as I didn't have a clue. Jessie confirmed it as her address which I passed onto the caller in agreement. It wasn't the callers' fault as there was nothing flagged on their system and I don't have a criminal record or similar history. If I were a lunatic though, they had just given me an address to target. I immediately worried about vulnerable people fleeing someone.

The telephone call progressed to assess Jessie's symptoms.

"Is she with you now?"

"No, she's in her bedroom."

"Has she been eating and drinking fine?"

"Yeah, though she may have drunk a little less than usual. She usually drinks plenty of water."

"Okay. Has her toilet frequency been the same?"

"Again slightly less than usual."

47

"Could you touch her skin and tell me if she feels hot or cold?"

"Yep. Okay, I'll check now." I said hastily opening my bedroom door to navigate to Jessie. Touching Jessie's skin was surprisingly warm, almost hot.

"She's rather warm."

"I see. That is to be expected. Could you check her eyes to see if they are fine?"

I stopped talking to take a close inspection of Jessie's eyes. Her right eye was bloodshot—a possible case of Conjunctivitis. The children and I had suffered through the condition a few years ago, which wasn't a pleasant experience, rather frightening for a child. I felt ashamed at not noticing her eyes earlier. I had been so focused on the spots that I didn't take the time to see.

"One of the eyes is bloodshot, like the onset of Conjunctivitis."

"Monitor the eye, from everything you've told me; I am certain that it is Chicken Pox. At this stage, your daughter should rest at home. Reassure her that she will be fine. It's very rare for there to be complications. The spots appear on most of her body when the blisters do burst that is when the itching becomes severe, and the spots spread. At this stage, she would be infectious. Try to put socks or something on her hands when she sleeps to stop her itching. Eventually, the spots will disperse after a week or two. Scratching the spots can leave permanent scars, so make sure she doesn't itch. Bedding and clothes should be washed on a high temperature to kill the germs. If her condition

48

worsens, you can call back again, and someone will be here to assist."

"Thank you."

The call disconnected. The health adviser wasn't concerned. Jessie just needed rest, and I had to monitor her and focus on her comfort.

"The doctor said you'll be fine. See, I told you not to worry. You'll feel the urge to itch, but we need to make sure you don't so that you get better quicker." I said with a smile.

I cuddled Jessie.

"Mums going to go crazy." Jessie worried.

"No, she won't. She only worries because she cares."

"She panics and makes me scared."

"I'm sure she'll be fine. Don't worry. Just focus on getting some rest."

Jessie didn't seem convinced, but I hoped that Casey would surprise her and not be so neurotic.

"I'll message mummy to let her know what's happening," I said as I left her room.

Casey often auto responds to every illness the same way regardless of severity or symptoms; Calpol and doctors. She never takes the time to monitor and reassure the children. In one way it's good that she is pro-active, but it comes at a cost. Jessie feels incredibly anxious when there's mention of the doctor or even Casey. She knows what she will do and how she reacts. It's sad that in a moment where she is the one suffering, she also contends with the weight of other peoples potential reactions. I don't like that at all. A child shouldn't have to worry about their parent's behaviour.

"Connor will make me look at the spots."

"No, he won't. Why would he do that?"

"He always does. If anything bothers someone, he forces them to face it."

"I'll have a word with mummy, so she knows, then he won't do it."

"She won't stop him, and he won't listen. He does what he wants."

"Well, he better not. I'm not putting up with that."

I am sick and tired of hearing about such damning behaviour. Casey doesn't correct Connor. She needs his money, and without that, she wouldn't have anything. Just be left up north with kids and no support. I guess he knows that too.

He has been a bane of contention for so long. Just looking at him, I can see a controlling manipulator who loves himself—placing himself above everyone else. For a long time, he had been talking negatively about me to Jessie and anyone that would listen, thinking I wouldn't know. Jessie however, tells me everything. He likes to put me down to raise himself but says nothing to me in person.

During a handover, a few weeks after court, I was ready to confront him. Jessie desperately wanted to avoid any arguing. For that journey, I took a family member to return Jessie while I waited in the car. My blood was boiling and heart rate increasing just being in proximity. My daughter had suffered for far too long, and I was fed-up standing by fighting the honest fight.

I bite my tongue for Jessie's sake, but sometimes I do raise my genuine concerns with Casey. She's defensive and oblivious to what goes on around her.

Communicating with Casey was an arduous task. She is incapable of being anything other than melodramatic. I am more philosophical, understanding that most bouts of infections heal on their own as the body naturally fights back. Medicine isn't always the cure. Casey wanted me to take Jessie to the hospital immediately. Even after I explained the advice, I had been given; she continued with her demands better safe than sorry.

I didn't humour her. I understood that she would be frustrated at not being in control, but I was more than capable of caring for our daughter.

My mum is a nurse at the nearby hospital; she is always available for advice. The 111 service is only a phone call away. They had already given me all the information I needed. The most important thing was to make sure that Jessie was comfortable. Her mother's anxiety is secondary. I kept her in the loop, respecting her role and opinions, but most of all, I listened to Jessie.

She was a trooper, a courageous girl. Jessie hated having spots on her body. They tormented her, yet she would do her best to cover them up and hardly complained. But, then they began to burst, and everything changed. I was thrust immediately into a war zone. Screams and hysterics boomed from wall to wall as the whaling erupted. Credit to her though she tried her best to cope with the torture, and I tried in vain to douse the pain with soothing creams to calm her skin and prevent the itching.

Usually, I say to Jessie when she has a cough or a cold "Are you okay? That's the best I can do." It makes us both laugh. Because of that, she thinks I don't know what to do when it comes to health, but the reality is that I am fine. Jessie could now see that for herself and pleased that I was there by her side. Calm, collected and responsive. I was doing everything advised, not missing a beat. The situation was under control. We both handled it well.

Then the situation turned on its head. The days were elapsing too fast, much faster than the speed of recovery. Jessie was due to return north with her mother. It was one of those rare occasions where she had planned to travel. At Jessie's request, I messaged Casey to try and change her return date so that she can recover at home with me. It made no sense to put her through such an arduous journey and risk her body, reacting to the spots in public.

Casey was adamant that Jessie will be returning on the planned date, no matter the circumstances. I was horrified and felt her decision was madness. She can't go back to school yet in any event; I couldn't understand the urgency. I had updated her regularly throughout as had Jessie.

As an alternative, I offered to drive Jessie rather than her having to switch trains for the journey north. It would be better if she had privacy and a comfortable permanent seat for the entirety of the trip. Again this was rebuffed. Casey would be coming as she was also collecting Emma from her holiday stay with the other side of the family. Not only was she placing Jessie at risk but the innocent general public. There was no care for the health or wellbeing of others. She was coming regardless, and Jessie would be returning with her.

The drive to the train station wasn't easy. The local station closed, so I had to make an extra thirty-minute drive to another station. Witnessing Jessie screaming in pain in the car was horrifying.

"YOU'RE HURTING ME. GET OFF ME. ARGH!"

She was shouting at the spots. If we were in public, then I'm sure she would've aroused suspicion about me. Her behaviour took me by surprise. She had been suppressing the pain so admirably throughout all of this time. Now that she was in the car travelling they must have caused her such discomfort. I was genuinely worried that the long journey for her would be excruciating.

Upon arriving at the train station, Casey immediately approached opening Jessie's car door. She was comforting and reassuring. It was a beautiful side of her to witness. She can often be like that in my presence to give me a false impression, but she seemed genuine. Jessie went with her mother and sister in tow. None of them seemed too pleased to be heading north but they travelled together. By all accounts, the journey hadn't been as bad as expected. Jessie had slept most of the trip, which helped take her mind from the pain and discomfort. Casey allowed Jessie to sit alongside her, even laying down which surprised me. Connor's parent's collected them from the station and took them home. Thankfully a long travel north wasn't as bad as it could've been, but for me, it wasn't worth the risk. There was no justification. Jessie was already being cared for successfully.

As Jessie was recuperating at home with her mother, I was becoming frustrated. Casey had promised Jessie plenty of niceties such as playing Monopoly together and watching movies. None of these happened, just lies to give her something positive to focus. I despise broken promises. It inspires mistrust. Something I don't want Jessie feeling is normal in life. How hard is it to play with your child?

8

DADDY

Certain people have had chapters dedicated to them, whether it be good or bad, but not me. So here I am, explaining me, flaws and all. I can be positive, bubbly, funny, and an overall joy to be around. Jessie loves my whimsical personality; I keep her entertained. She also likes the other side of my personality. I don't put up with nonsense and will stand up for those I love by taking on the world. Jessie doesn't say it, but I can see it in her eyes; she is proud of her dad. She does offer a platitude of "Love You's".

Jessie randomly proposes, desiring me to be her husband. I always find it strange and explain that she doesn't need to as I will always be here, and she will fall in love with someone one day. In fairness to Casey, she hates my darker side. I can be abrupt and obnoxious, maybe. Stress certainly brings out the worst, only when provoked. If I'm working on a project, then I thrive under pressure. Casey often said, "You're the biggest hothead I have ever met". Of course, I didn't see it because I'm on the other side of that. I know all of the little things which trigger my frustrations and anger, and it was often Casey. Aside from Jessie leaving I have thrived on my own. Time apart has allowed me to connect deeper within myself. I know what I enjoy and the sparks that irritate. Reducing those negatives enable me to breathe easily and keep that positive personality at the forefront.

In all honesty, I like who I am. Just think of me like the Incredible Hulk. The nerdy scientist, funny and charismatic, but not vulnerable. People don't walk over me, I won't allow it, and they certainly would never be free to walk over Jessie now or in her adult years.

An example of my stubbornness is a football (soccer) match I played in my early twenties. I started the game in the centre of midfield and doing okay, but the pitbull of a bloke in defence who happened to be the captain kept shouting, "Get back, get back!", but the guy next to me was also screaming, "Go forward, get forward!" This blew my mind. I didn't care how tough the people were around me; I am no one's whipping boy, so I started losing control shouting back at everyone. The manager subbed me, but later in the match, he needed me back on the pitch. I reacted, shouting, "You can fuck off; I'm not going back on." It was only a pre-season friendly game, and my first match with the team, which would also be my last. In training I had run rings around the players. They called me *White Pele*, which was an honour as the real Pele is up there with the Messi's of this world. If only they could've shown that same respect during a game. I've never taken football seriously, only for fun and enjoyment.

Playing in muddy fields in the rain wasn't as appealing as practicing skills in the summer. I enjoy kick-ups and shifting the ball to my chest, shoulder and incorporating headers. I would focus on my weakest ability to make myself better. I became able with both feet and perfected free kicks like David Beckham, but unlike him, I wouldn't be doing so under pressure in high-intensity matches, but at the park aiming for goalposts and the crossbar. Smashing the ball cleanly against the frame of the goal for me was the same as Beckham scoring his game-winning free kicks.

This perfectionist attitude holds me in good stead throughout my life. I have a deep understanding of computing with courses completed at college and university, skilled in web-design and a competent writer which has come naturally to me since before I can remember. I can't say that I took writing seriously at school. I do, however, remember writing a beautiful story in Primary School but the contents have long since forgotten.

The time in High School was distracted by my love of Sports and Computers. English wasn't high on my list of interests. I now know why, and it's only taken me to the age of 37 to figure out the reason. I don't often pursue skills which come naturally to me. I have always taken the path of learning something new, almost alien. Computers were in their infancy when I became interested. They were basic with nothing more than a green flashing text alert. They soon evolved into these complicated machines. My curiosity was peaked, and in time I would build computers, and also repair them whenever there was a fault. Web-design became the new technological advancement which again I had to pursue. Initially, it was beyond my understanding, but I never stopped learning and experimenting. Now I am competent with multiple websites to my name with a deep understanding of the design process, administration and sever knowledge.

I have gone full-circle embracing my natural talent to write. Time gives us the opportunity to reflect on our paths in life. I have tested myself enough to know that anything I apply my mind to can be overcome. I'm not lazy, nor do I lack intelligence. A fast learner but only if it is a subject of interest. Put flowers in front of me and ask me to learn the name of each then I will fall asleep and lose concentration. I understand my strengths and flaws. I'm not perfect, but I am loyal and honest.

Regardless of all the skills I have learned and accomplished, Jessie is my most significant achievement. My perseverance to overcome difficulties and master the unknowns pales in significance to her. Throughout court proceedings, I learnt a lot at every stage. I was hands-on throughout writing all of my statements and liaising with legal advisors. Jessie knows that daddy is intelligent, determined and not scared to take on the world. No stone was left unturned in my pursuit to bring her home, and she knows that no one could've done more. Unjustly or unfairly as it is, it would seem that the outcome was our fate. You can't bend destiny, but that doesn't mean that it is how we will have to live forever. Time apart was needed to reveal our true love and learn about ourselves during adversity. I like to take positives from negatives, how else can we evolve and learn?

I am bitter about the situation. It should never have happened and the behaviour of Casey acting the victim still to this day not only irritates me but it's disrespectful and absolutely not in Jessie's best interests. We should be collecting and returning her between homes, not at public locations. She acts the victim in all of this but in Court I had her dad storm towards me, and since then her boyfriend has threatened me. Not once have I physically threatened or gestured to any of them, so which one of us should be scared? I'm not afraid of any of them. If I can tell a big brute to, "Fuck off." Then I can hold my own against these bullies.

Positive people bring out the best in me, and negative the worst. I'm not a pushover, but I'm also not a bully. With respect, I reciprocate. Casey knows my personality, so she also knows how to stir the fire inside of me to get a reaction. In this case, she always uses Jessie. I would fight an entire army for her, and she knows it too, so she plays her games to make me appear unhinged. If being a protective father is a crime, then I am guilty as charged.

9

CHAOS

It was obvious to me that Jessie had been prevented from messaging recently. Usually she would send messages throughout the day, but this became rarer. A voice recording she had sent alarmed me. It was apparent that Jessie was whispering as to not be heard by anyone else. She said "I love you. See you soon." Beggars belief that she can't send me such an expression with confidence. Instead felt the need to be secretive so that no-one else knows.

I had tried to help Casey with sharing my TV subscriptions as Jessie complained that she doesn't have the same shows to watch when she is with her mother. Casey tried to be diplomatic but wasn't interested in my offer. We don't agree on much, and I don't suppose we ever will.

Casey suggested that Jessie has plenty to watch but spends most of her time in the garden with friends or they are out. I knew that this was a lie. Jessie regularly complains to me that Emma doesn't play with her, and always sulking and miserable. They hardly go anywhere as a family. It's a humdrum life with nothing eventful planned.

I offered my advice on viewing content for what it was worth. TV channels are more suitable than online social media content. Jessie like most kids is obsessed with trending apps but they are rarely monitored. I understand that too much TV is anti-social and requires monitoring. Jessie isn't one to watch TV mindlessly and do nothing else. She will always make time to play, write, read and be with friends. To that end she doesn't need restrictions but Casey explained that she limits TV exposure and monitors online content which I doubted. Emma doesn't have many friends. She's struggled to adapt to the upheaval and dramatic change of lifestyle. Limiting her TV viewing doesn't make sense, from what I have heard she suffers with depression and an identity crisis. Surely it's better to watch TV than self-loathing and obsessing on her phone. Of course Casey won't say any of that to me. She likes to portray the perfect family.

I explain that I allow Jessie to do what she wants. I don't limit anything unless I feel I have to intervene. Instead prefer to allow her freedom to make her own choices. One of the kids she plays with apparently is nasty and manipulative. I would limit her involvement with that kid. Nasty influences and bullies are more damaging than TV.

Any topic between me and Casey soon erupts into drama. I had been messaging Jessie, and had my suspicions that Casey had been restricting her communications with me.

Why on earth would you ask a 9 year old such a manipulative and pressuring message "Wasn't you allowed to text earlier".

Stop exaggerating and trying to fight all the time. I'm not getting dragged into arguments anymore. It was an innocent question. I never pushed it further. I've allowed unrestricted contact for a long time. It's how it should be.

How am I exaggerating. She's 9 years old…

Casey is great at acting the perfect parent. Does her best to try and make me feel inferior to her wisdom. Full of insight and answers however for seven years she was almost missing from Jessie's life. Now she feels she knows everything. I felt no other choice but to respond.

Your very controlling and rather manipulative. Constantly twisting everything onto me. I allow Jessie to be free. She knows I only care about her happiness and never worry about me. I can't ask any questions without it being a crime. Just because you say something doesn't necessarily make it true. When she is 12 she'll be coming home. I'll take all the hits and accusations until then. It's absolutely fine.

The next morning I received a mountain of missed calls from Casey. It was clear that she was ready to mount a war. I figured us talking in that moment would only end up making matters worse. It was best that we don't speak.

Casey began to take a keen interest in Jessie's interactions with me. Not only monitoring our messages but sitting close to her listening into our conversations. It annoyed me that

Jessie couldn't talk in private. When she's surrounded by everyone else the goofy and electric energy that radiates from her is extinguished. Chats become cumbersome, serious and less engaging. Casey is controlling and suffers from paranoia.

On this occasion Jessie informed me via Whats App that she can't receive photos anymore as her mum had changed her phone settings. My response was one of shock and questioned her mothers motives.

I can't receive photos or videos because mum stopped it.
She is annoying
Love you

    Doesn't surprise me. Some people allow jealousy and being controlling to cloud their judgement. Never thought it would last. Probably stop messages soon. It's been like this for way to long. I have to fight for everything. Love you too.

Mum reads these texts
You Know

    I know

Love you more

    Love you forever and ever

Unbeknown to me at the time, Casey had been sitting with Jessie when the message was received. Doesn't change anything to me. I would never say anything to Jessie that I wouldn't say in her mothers presence. It would be easier if I could say it directly but she doesn't cope with questions or criticism. The message I sent was blown out of proportion. Casey launched a tirade of abuse at me. I was outraged and sent a strong message of my own in reply. Every bit of frustration and hate I felt towards her came through in each word.

How absolutely dare you make Jessie cry. She is so angry that you belittled me in a text. She's been crying for over 10 minutes now. It's disgusting absolutely vile what you just said to her on a text message.

Go to hell you're a lunatic. Read the messages. I've said nothing wrong. Your the control freak that stopped her receiving photos. Broken promises of regular horse riding. Loves it the first time then tells me you won't let her ever go again. Your a psycho.

Jessie later told me that Casey had cried for more than two hours after our argument. I don't have any feeling towards her. I can only guess that the tears were due to a realisation that every day that goes by Jessie is closer to coming home to me. She can't be held hostage forever. Maybe my book *A Father's Daughter* hits a nerve that causes distress. I don't mention the book to her so that's for her to deal with. I do know that she has either read the book or someone's told her parts as she did call me a *narcissist* recently. Not a word she would know or think to use. Evident to me that she knows the word I use for her and trying to use it on me. Hardly original to use someone else's term but it doesn't bother me either way as I am comfortable with myself. Casey's response was typical, nasty and continuing the same campaign of lies about the life we had together. I think she does it to hurt me and use as evidence were we to end up back at court. She probably thinks, by saying I was abusive then it happened. Yet in court her claims were thrown out. The messages continued to arrive.

Hell was living with you so no thanks. Never realised a person like you could exist manipulating emotionally controlling abusive sicko. You have made a 9-year old cry disgusting behaviour for an adult you are like a child yourself you don't care who you offend. Jessie hates your book she's crying about it and doesn't want to read it but you pressure her to. You are an absolute narcissist you should get help. This is over now that's it. I gave you a chance and now you are done.

Your just controlling. Find what I done wrong. Your the narcissist. It was always going to stop as you don't like people to talk freely. Talk to Jessie and actually find out what is upsetting her. You'll be surprised to find it's you.

She was clearly threatening to stop Jessie and I messaging via Whats App which validates what I was saying about her wanting to stop our contact. I'm used to her nonsense, vilifying me and reducing our previous life together to nothing but contempt. I was upset by the book remarks. It hurt deeply. Jessie hadn't shown me any distress or hate about the book. If it upsets her then I will immediately unpublish. Whilst writing *A Father's Daughter* is my most significant accomplishment it doesn't come before Jessie. I needed to talk to her to find out how she truly feels.

Jessie had a rare sleepover at her friends house that evening on the same day. Against the orders of her mother she video called me from her friends bedroom. I wasn't expecting the call and didn't instigate or request. Accepting the call allowed us to have a chat and for me to find out how she's feeling. She informed me that she doesn't hate my book. The reason she cried earlier was because Casey shut the bedroom door and ambushed Jessie. Accusing her of reading my book. When Jessie denied reading, Casey continued to accuse her of lying. It was her that made Jessie cry. She is absolutely vial. I can categorically say that Jessie has never read my book. The only chapters she has heard are *Author's Note* and *Jessie*. A lovely part dedicated to her. None of those contents were inappropriate.

I believe that Casey messaged me to say that I made her cry for two reasons.

1. Casey knows that I would do anything for Jessie. It is her only way to get me to unpublish *A Father's Daughter*.
2. Evidence gathering.

Casey believes by saying something out loud she can rely on that message as evidence against me. If that's the case then she is naive to think that Jessie wouldn't be questioned for her version of events. As she gets older, her voice holds more weight. Casey isn't fooling anyone.

Our video call only listed a few minutes. I encouraged Jessie to focus on her friend and have a good time. It's not fair for her friend to sit idly by while we chat. There was the other issue of her mother not approving of the call. I didn't want Jessie to get into trouble when she returns to her mother the next day. We said our love yous and the call ended. She was very cheeky to call me, but obviously felt the desire as soon as she was clear of her mothers controlling grasp.

10

OBSESSION

There is an unhealthy obsession of me by Casey and Connor. I had thought by now that they would've moved forward with their lives. I would expect them to be head over heels in love considering they are engaged and apparently due to get married, though I do have my suspicions that it will never happen.

Jessie has told me that they have secret meetings in their bedroom whereby they constantly talk about me. Whilst they think that they are whispering and talking in private, the reality is both girls can hear their conversations. Most of the time Jessie laughs it off with Emma. I'm sure Emma enjoys hearing Connor annoyed as she hates him with a passion. Knowing that I get under his skin probably brings her some joy and comfort.

Recently Emma was asleep and Jessie was awake alone listening. She had had enough.

"STOP TALKING ABOUT MY DAD!" She yelled in frustration.

Soon the conversation stopped. Casey and Connor entered Jessie's bedroom to confront her on the outburst. What happened at this moment is vague as we only spoke about it briefly. At some point, Casey left the room and Connor stayed behind to have a private word with Jessie.

"Do you know who you are talking to?" Connor threatened.

"Yeah, I do," Jessie responded with courage and certainty. She was done being the frightened little girl.

Her confidence made Connor uncomfortable. He hadn't witnessed her stand up to him before. Emma was becoming a natural at fighting back but Jessie prefers peace. She was probably learning from Emma. The situation had reached boiling point within Jessie as these meetings had become increasingly frequent. The bitterness and accusations had been happening for years, since the moment she arrived in Liverpool. There is a point in everyone when we feel enough is enough. For Jessie, this was that moment. Her dad wasn't here to speak up for himself so his little girl would be there for him. She fought for me as I do her. I couldn't be more proud, though I wish the situation hadn't required such a brave act. Why they continue to obsess about me can only point to jealousy and self-doubt. Taking their insecurities out on me.

If it weren't for Jessie, I would never think of them again. I'm stuck in their head while in my life I move on without them. To make matters worse Jessie had said that Connor intended to meet me at a recent handover. Have a friendly chat and shake hands putting the past behind us all, moving forward amicably. I have no interest in talking or shaking his hand. I don't need or want his approval. Rather strange that he would desire that, yet continue to speak negatively of me behind my back. Two-faced possibly come to mind. I don't suffer fools easily so he may as well go and play his game somewhere else. My only interest is collecting and returning Jessie. There is no need for Connor and me to be near one another.

.

11

DISRUPTION

Jessie was due to spend a few days home with me on October 2019, for the school half-term holiday. Casey had relayed a message that she would travel and bring Jessie. Saves me a journey for a change. With this in mind, I had the car repaired. The heavy mileage causes constant problems with the performance of the vehicle.

Whenever Casey travels she tends to cover both journeys. All in the benefit of Emma of course. She hates living up north, constantly craving to return home. Unlike Jessie, Emma has no form of transport back. I have offered in the past, but it simply falls on deaf ears. Either Casey endures the travel South again, or the grandfather returns her. Either way, I assumed that Jessie would return with them.

Transpires that my assumption was misplaced. I was required to return her. This irritated me. Not the fact that I travel. I'm used to that. A few years of the same routines becomes second nature. I get irritated by the fact that Casey will go the extra mile for Emma. She has travelled the entire journey just for her before, but not once has she ever done the journey for Jessie. She likes to make me think she does it to help but the entire reason is simple - Emma. She is the goddess in Casey's life. Will always come first. Jessie is second best. Thankfully for her, she has me. A father utterly dedicated, and that is something that both Casey and Emma envy. They wish for the same from their fathers.

The travel disruption almost caused Jessie not to come home for the holidays. I was determined not to prolong her anxiety any longer than necessary. Lord knows I would love to teach Casey a lesson and make her sweat. No way was Jessie suffering for lessons to be learnt. I was prepared to throw my body on the line yet again to return Jessie as required. The issue I had was money. I couldn't afford the travel. Mum stepped up yet again as she has always done. Like I had said to Jessie "She's never let us down yet." I did make her aware that mum had done more than enough for us. If she can help she will, but we can't take it for granted. The day when my life is in perfect order and able to finance the journeys can't come soon enough. Deep down I know that it's not reasonable to expect to be able to venture so far as often as I do for much longer. My body suffers, but that's not the problem. How many people could afford to travel so far consistently? It comes at an incredible expense.

Relocating and residing nearby would be an option to consider but I know that Casey is unpredictable. At any moment she could spontaneously relocate. A sudden argument with Connor could spark an instant reaction. She doesn't think of the kids lives and turmoil just trying to manage the torment of her mind. There will be a day when

Jessie is home, and that day gets ever closer. The situation can't last forever. The most important factor is that Jessie simply doesn't like being up north. It's a reprieve coming home to me to the town she was raised and loves. Moving closer would only alienate her from the life she adored.

A discrepancy to resolve is *arriving at six,* unclear whether that is AM or PM. A twelve-hour time gap between them. Nigh on impossible to be punctual and present without being informed prior. I couldn't be arriving at the train station at six o'clock in the morning if she's arriving in the evening. Like-wise I wouldn't want to be in bed in the morning if Jessie is waiting for me. The train station continues to be the location of exchange as it has been for the past few years. Ridiculous and unnecessary but Casey can't get over herself. Seeming to take solace from believing her web of lies. Quite frankly I've given up playing her games. I just allow her to continue the facade and focus on Jessie.

Jessie sent me a photo and a lovely exchange of messages on Whats App while I await confirmation of the evening or morning collection.

You Always put a smile on my face

Me Too

I love you

The photo was bland with Jessie not showing much desire to smile or appearing particularly happy. I worried about her emotional wellbeing in her mothers care. She seems lost and void of the spark that radiates in my care. Of course it could just be a typically stressful day from school. Knowing her mindset I knew it was a deeper issue.

So sweet. Love you too. I think when you come home we should spend a day in silence. Don't talk to each other. See how long we can last. Oh the fun.

That's impossible. I always talk to you.

Love you too 'smiley' you don't look excited. Boring day? I'm feeling a bit nutty. I know we won't last 2 mins. Haha. In that video your not moving you mouth fast enough. Gotta be the song. Really fight it.

OK
(Smiling photo attached)

The lady of few words. The dreaded OK

Your so annoying

(Strange smiling photo attached)
See crazy (crazy emoji)

Weird person

(Laughing emoji)

Maybe but your very much like me so…

I'm going on tik tok now bye love you

How dare you. OK lovey have fun.

Thanks

A typical message exchange between Jessie and I. We regularly show love and have a fair bit of banter. When she's away from me she becomes slightly more serious. Suppressing so much inside which I don't like her enduring. We get to communicate though, so at least we have that to keep us going.

I had done my best to avoid Casey for almost two months. Handover exchanges were done from the car. Jessie would walk a few yards herself back into her mothers care, and I collected her from school. As time goes on I've learnt not to respond to messages. It never ends well, and not worth the agro. Then a few days before the autumn half-term holidays were due to commence, I received a text message. Casey was putting her demands on me, then trying her best to manipulate my responses. I didn't take the bait, and blocked her immediately. She can play her games, but I will have no part in it.

Next week I'll be taking Jessie to the train station, on Monday 21st 6pm. You can bring her back anytime Thursday 24th before 8pm as she has a 2 day brownies trip on Friday 25th, she needs a good sleep Thursday night so she's not too tired to go and I have prep to do before she travels. So Thursday is best for her return home.

What I should mention is that Casey and I already had this conversation a few months ago. At the time she was acting diplomatic, while just making up all the rules. I know for a fact that Jessie is going to Brownies in the evening Friday. There is no rush to get her back earlier than Friday.

If you had to live with the limited contact Jessie and I have you'd understand why I fight so hard for every inch. 6pm is later than expected. The loss of a day. If Jessie's content with returning Thursday then I will do but if she wants to soak up as much time possible I don't see how Friday morning would hurt. I'm not pressuring or influencing. Whatever she wants.

Bring her back Thursday she is travelling with brownies Friday morning. It's non negotiable bringing her back Friday will ruin her social trip with brownies.

Never is negotiable. You don't get to order me about. The order states split holidays. You get 4 days with both weekends. The Monday is late. Within my rights to do Friday but like I say I will respect what Jessie wants.

Thursday no later than 8 PM brining her back Friday will ruin her trip so thats fine if you want to ruin the start of her first brownies trip that's on you. You can add that to your book. I'm trying here but you always have to create emotional distress by Jessie under pressure.

Casey always twists everything onto me. At no point did I refuse to return her Thursday. I simply said I will leave Jessie to decide. She wouldn't miss the event either way. She was just trying to fuel the fire by making me seem a monster. I had grown tired of her antics. Casey always has the last word as she messages something spiteful then blocks for a few days so she doesn't have to read my response. I sent a message in reply and then blocked her. Not to teach her lesson. Simply put, I can't be bothered with her anymore. I have better things to do than communicate with *her.*

I've already said whatever Jessie wants. Stop being manipulative. You twist everything. I ignore recently as I can't be bothered with the nonsense anymore. This is my last message.

The arguing was crazy as they were just leaving for a short weekend family break to a caravan park. Deciding to engage me at that moment didn't make any sense. I had agreed with Casey for Jessie to go with her, and that I'll see her after. She had to go and ruin it. Knowing her, her mood will be painful all weekend. I only defended myself. She's the one on a warpath. I was more than fair when we spoke a few months ago. She's the one regularly moving goalposts, and exerting her will on everyone. I for one, won't ever bow to her. If she learnt to be respectful then their wouldn't need to be animosity. The issue I had was Casey bringing Jessie at 6 PM. She usually arrives in the morning. I had agreed to her travelling with that in mind. We already had a limited holiday, taking away the Monday too was a step too far. I was fighting to spend quality time with Jessie.

To my surprise Jessie messaged me almost instantly after my message was sent to Casey. There was no other way for her to relay her message. Jessie was her only avenue of dialogue remaining. When Connor or anyone else is present, Casey likes to act tough and over step the mark. Most likely goaded to react and be the boss. It never works with me. I refused to let Jessie suffer though. She should be enjoying the holiday not witnessing fighting. I hadn't made her aware. It was Casey putting the weight of everything on our nine year old daughter.

Daddy you need to bring me back on Thursday because I want to go brownies pls

Whatever you decide, just enjoy your weekend and have fun (smiley emoji)

OK

Love You

Love You

A diplomatic response that would put Jessie's mind at ease but leave Casey with questions. Until Jessie is in my care I won't know what she really wants to do regarding the return journey. Often she is influenced by Casey, making her feel anxious.

12

AUTUMN

Casey's recent behaviour and manipulation annoyed me enough that I had others accompany me to collect Jessie from the train station. Upon arriving Casey was standing by the side of the car park with Emma and Jessie. I positioned my car close but not directly next to her. She knows my car. As Jessie tried to pull away, Casey held her back.

"Not yet. Wait."

I was confused. Jessie has previously walked to my car fine. I didn't want to engage with Casey, and it was obvious that she wanted to see me. By contrast, I couldn't get far enough away from her. My mum and nephew David-James had accompanied me.

"David, could you go and get Jessie for me?" I asked.

"Sure." He said appearing confused about the need.

Jessie was only a few feet away from the car. More than capable of walking to us without any concerns. Casey was playing her game so I just used one of the cards available to me. She wouldn't be getting an audience with me today. I foiled her tactic.

Jessie entered the car and made herself comfortable in the front seat.

"Are you okay?" I asked.

"Yeah. Mum was confused that you didn't collect me. Emma spoke to me on the way down, but mum didn't bother." She said.

"At least you got to talk to Emma," I reassured.

"Mum hugged me when you arrived. She wouldn't let me go. It was weird. She never hugs."

"Must be nice to get a hug though?"

"It just felt weird. Mum's waiting for Emma's dad to collect her."

"Emma's dad's taking her to nannies?"

"Yeah. Mum said she's going to make him stop at the ATM to get money for the cost of Emma's train ticket."

"Good luck with that. He doesn't like giving money. Cheeky though, to get him to help out then order him about."

"Granddad didn't want to come and get her."

"Why wouldn't he get her?"

"I don't think he wants to be near you."

This had me laughing. These people are psychos. They hate me for fighting for Jessie and writing *A Father's Daughter*. I wonder what they wish I did instead. Role over, and just let my daughters life be chaos. Never get to see her father again. Live with her mother accusing me of abuse to anyone that would listen. I am sure that it would make them happy, but, my daughter deserves so much better. She shouldn't have to live with those fabricated stories nor should she have to live a life away from her father. We are the innocents. Hate me all they like. It's their behaviour that needs to be improved.

For the rest of the short journey home, we shared laughs and banter which took us a million miles away from the bitterness between families. Jessie enjoyed an ice-lolly at my mums home and then we returned David-James and thanked him for taking up his time to aid me for the handover. While his attendance was only briefly required it made an incredible difference. If it weren't for him or my mum in attendance, I would've had to deal with Casey myself. For now, I can't be near her. She agitates me too much. My nephews sacrifice of his time is appreciated.

Jessie never wants to sleep, she keeps me up until the late hours, watching movies, talking, and anything that interests her. With our time together limited I give in to those requests. When the morning arrives she expects me up as soon as her eyes open. Sometimes I am awake before her but when the roles are reversed she doesn't give me a moment's peace. Even trying to role me off the bed. I embrace the antics and often try my best to delay the morning rise by pretending to get up, only to then lay back down throwing the covers back over. A few seconds of victory before Jessie piles on calling me cheeky. I can do this a few times before she loses patience.

When Jessie is home with me, Casey and her family try to break the moment up at every opportunity. The granddad barely communicates with Jessie while in her mothers care. It's rare for him to bother at all, but miraculously within a single day of arriving home to me, the phone rings. Jessie isn't impressed with him and decides for herself not to engage. His intentions are not lost on her while Casey also inundates with constant messages. Trivial topics such as a treat when she returns. The conversation could easily wait until she gets back seeing as we barely get quality time together. The reality is that Casey's goal is disruption. She does not want Jessie to settle and enjoy our time together without a bit of interference. Again most of the time, Jessie doesn't wish to communicate.

Jessie never misses a beat at lunch. By all accounts, her mother doesn't provide her with lunch but with me, she knows I will. If I lose track of time she will be ready to complain and usher me towards the direction of the kitchen. We had an enjoyable walk to the local shops. Jessie told me more about her life up north. She always has much on her mind, wanting to get off her chest and be free from the torment. I listen intently, supportive and understanding.

Upon entering the shop the first thing I hear is "Can I?" as Jessie points excitedly at the sprinkled doughnuts. She knows my response, it never changes. Always the same.

"Go on then," I said with a smile.

She doesn't expect a treat as she isn't demanding. If I couldn't get it for her she wouldn't sulk. It's this compassionate side to her personality that makes me want to provide her with everything. We popped out to the shops to gather food for lunch and snacks for an evening movie night. Easy for us to over-do-it, with crisps, chocolate and popcorn. On this occasion, we showed restraint. Well, actually it was me exerting control. Crisps, drink and sweets were enough. Popcorn was a stretch too far. If she were home for an extended period then I would've obliged but consuming so many snacks in a short period cant be good for either of us.

Jessie recently got herself a boyfriend. I find it adorable. I don't pester her or try to make her anxious. I want her to be a confident woman when she is all grown up and that starts with her first boyfriends. She has had little crushes before. Always gaining boys attention but she seems to like this one more than any other before. I noticed her writing in her notepad but left her alone to her musings.

"Do you know why I respect you?" Jessie asked.

"Respect me? What do you mean?" I responded.

"Connor always interferes, winding me up, looking at everything I write. You don't. You give me space."

"He shouldn't be doing that. Just ignore him. He sounds like an idiot. What you write is your business."

Jessie raised a smile, and we hugged. I never check her notes or phone messages. She's only allowed to have close friends and family contacts. It's important to me that Jessie has her independence and feels trusted. I expect her to come to me directly should anything be said that is untoward or causes her concern. She knows that I am always available.

Lord knows Jessie spends most of her time doing the same things up north. Indoors or trampoline with friends, and repeat. When she's home with me she attaches herself to the life she misses. Chooses to absorb our home, making the most of the surroundings. I often worry that she will miss fun opportunities and memories to create. Last time she was home I took her to a firework show. Nice for her to be outside enjoying the sky illuminate with such spectacle.

With one day remaining until I am due to return her. We agreed to go swimming. This had us both excited. A regular source of fun and silly antics. I can't remember a single time where we've been and not enjoyed ourselves. This time was no different. For a long time, we've had to share the same changing room which had driven me crazy for longer than I can remember. She was just too insecure to be on her own. Now she was getting older, confident and fine with changing independently. We had adjoining cubicles. While we were changing into our swimming costumes I could hear moaning in frustration. Jessie was getting herself all worked up. I laughed as I find over dramatics funny. "Relax, there's no rush," I assured her while trying to keep the laughing to myself.

We were soon ready for swimming and walked towards the pool with haste. Neither of us dragging behind as we ebbed ever closer to the water. I don't know why but Jessie hesitated by the side of the pool. I wasted no time getting in and immediately complained about the cold temperature. After a short while, my body adjusted and it wasn't so bad, but that initial transition was unbearable. Jessie soon joined me in the pool. For a long time in her life, she couldn't swim. My brother-in-law Lee took some time last year to help and encourage her. I'm not a prolific swimmer myself, often messing about in the lessons at school as I had no genuine interest. I was happy enough to simply jump in and out of the pool making massive splashes. For me that was fun. As I got older I learnt myself and now I can do as much as I want. Even now I can be lazy but able to float for extended periods and swim the distances I desire. It was important that Jessie is taught by someone confident and proficient.

A few months later she had lessons at school. Lee had set the groundwork for Jessie to then thrive and continue learning. She was now an able swimmer, only a few meters but it's enough for us to dominate the shallow end of the pool. I never let her go beyond her chin standing flat-footed. She grows fast so we check her height in the pool to decide boundaries.

Jessie instantly decided to attack me. Jumping on my back like a wild lunatic. A few steps forward had me to my knees, weighing me down, torturing my back and legs. She was amused at the sight of me wading with my head just above the water and her clinging on for a ride. I held on the side of the wall as I faced forward away from the water. Then swayed all the way to my right to bash Jessie gently into the pool wall. The same again the other side. I did this a few times to try and shake her off. Clearly the antics between us had started without delay.

When the time came to return Jessie on Thursday as Casey had requested, she hesitated. Jessie didn't want to leave. The few days together was far too short, and not what Jessie had anticipated. Casey arriving with her so late on Monday meant that we practically lost that day together. To travel on Thursday was another day lost. We only had two full days together for a holiday of which she only gets a few per year.

Casey gets to see Jessie almost every day, but by contrast, we barely get to see each other. No matter how much I try to make Casey understand, it always falls on deaf ears. She never takes the time to see it from other peoples perspective.

Jessie wanted me to delay her return until Friday morning; however, I had previously agreed to return Thursday before the arguing. Rather than give Casey this moment to use against me in any future court hearings, I adhered to our agreement. In future, I would be more critical of the finer details of travel before confirming. Had I known how late Casey would arrive then I would've declined and done the travelling myself. Our time together is crucial. Casey may not understand that, but Jessie and I do.

13

CONTROLLING

Casey had been late to arrive for the scheduled return of Jessie from our half-term holiday together. It was surprising as it was her demanding Thursday against my pleas for a Friday travel. Night covered the park in darkness. We relocated to the other side where Casey would arrive. Efficient, safer and more comfortable for Jessie. David-James accompanied Jessie into the mothers care while I waited in the car nearby. According to him, Connor's embrace of Jessie was anything but pleasant.

"Why are you here and not over there!" He said, abruptly in disdain.

I could only imagine how uncomfortable Jessie would have felt at that moment. I wish I had been there myself. My daughter isn't responsible for what I decide. If he has an issue then he should take it up with me. It would be nice to know why I can't simply drop Jessie off at their home like normal separated parents. An arrogant and self-righteous individual, unable to exert even a modicum of compassion. He seems comfortable to act like the gatekeeper, yet doesn't accompany Casey and the kids on any journey South. Hardly protective or nurturing. When Casey and I were together it's not a journey I would've expected her to travel alone. I hardly care now, but it does reflect either his character or the contempt her family has towards him. Whatever the reason it's hardly endearing.

Hearing of the situation angered me immensely on the journey home. I had driven past him to park the car prior. The smugness and god-like posture he exerted had me amused. I couldn't help but nod my head laughing as I drove past. The kids have an intense dislike of him and Casey seems to keep her distance at every opportunity. Hardly the warm, charming and wonderful upgrade.

His obsession with me is sweet, but I can only imagine it coming from jealousy. I have something he doesn't possess - charisma. A people person, whimsical, compassionate, random, goofy, and creative. No two moments are the same and Jessie comes alive when I am with her. From all accounts, she hides her torment, and those close to her up north don't get to see the real Jessie. Instead; sullen, lonely and lost at home when her friends are not with her. Without them, she would suffer greatly. I worry for her every day, but each of those days is a step closer to her return. We remain strong and steadfast in our resolve to right the wrongful decision which keeps her prisoner in a place and life she never wanted.

I had tried recently to minimise my presence during Jessie's return to her mother after our contacts together. I don't like being near any of them. Preferring to keep my life tranquil.

Negativity radiates from them which isn't good for one's sanity. I would attend the next handover. It shouldn't be hard for Jessie to transition smoothly from one parent to another. Casey is robotic, lacking an emotional connection. Connor's priority is himself, so in there lies the problem. Jessie doesn't come first for any of them. Thankfully for her, she does with me.

My daughter's life in her mothers care is alarming, and truly frightening. Casey bombards her with endless questions about our time together. An interrogation which borders on abuse. Jessie is routinely left in tears trying to fight off question after question, terrified to return. Casey's dark and twisted mind is revealed in the messages she sends me. Accusing me of upsetting Jessie. Blaming me for the endless tears. Yet I was 250 miles away. It is her behaviour which causes so much distress. The blame doesn't solely lie with the mother. Her boyfriend is a controlling, obsessive and manipulative bully. I have explained to Jessie the need for her to speak to her teacher or pass her notes she has written if she feels frightened when I am not there to protect her. I won't allow her to be a helpless victim.

Connor recently informed Jessie that he has found my social media profiles. An obvious attempt to annoy Jessie, but more importantly, get a reaction from me. From day one, I have noticed that he craves attention. An elitist believing himself to be higher in society. My daughter deserves so much better.

14

PSYCHIC

Following on from the psychic reading immediately after Jessie's abduction in 2017. There have been a couple of readings, one with a psychic in Harlow, Essex specialising in communicating with spirits. The other by the original psychic when my mum bumped into her randomly. It's understandable that some people aren't believers and sceptical. I, however, have heard too much to discount anything. I don't expect everything to happen that I am told but I believe most *will*. That is my opinion. My step-dad was sceptical when he was alive. He wouldn't give any time to listen to anything paranormal beyond the realm of what we understand. Yet in a psychic reading since he passed away he has come through to communicate. Rather ironic but reassuring to know that our loved ones don't simply disappear at the end of their life cycle. It gives me comfort and solace that there could be an after life. For a long time I never thought it possible. I was a cynic myself.

Jessie will definitely be coming home to live with you at the age of twelve or just after. Sal was absolute in her assessment. This fits

91

perfectly with my expectations and intentions to continue fighting to get justice in providing the life that Jessie has always desired. During the other psychic reading with Bob a year ago he had mentioned that my step-dad had recently crossed over to the other realm. Apparently, it does take time. Their energy is stronger the longer they have transitioned. At the time he couldn't give a timeline or be definitive on Jessie's situation. There was mention that both sides; Casey and I were locked in a bitter battle, with neither relinquishing. This heated exchange made progress impossible. My step-dad would be working on his end to help. I didn't understand what this meant but Bob explained that if a spirit says that, then it means a lot. With Sal now confident that the outcome will be favourable, it does demonstrate progress.

Through Bob, my step-dad made reference to me getting married and laughing. I didn't understand what he meant. The only thing I can take from it is that I couldn't be further from being married that he found it amusing. I just wished I could've completely understood what he was trying to say so that I could connect and acknowledge what was being said. I was only sitting in on my mums reading as I had driven her the journey there.

He adored the family dog 'Rustler'. Saved from a terrible life when Casey and I fostered him for a local dog rescue. My parents adopted him and he has been a mainstay in all of our lives. During my mums reading he told us to cut the dogs hair as he can't see clearly and need to feed him more. Always looking out for the dog. He was incredibly bonded with him. Rustler would often lay alongside and give comfort during his final moments, possibly sensing his frailty and need for a companion.

"He is trying to communicate around the home. As he has only recently departed he doesn't have the strength to control it yet," Bob explained

All of us had noticed strange phenomena in our own homes regularly since his passing. Even in the car journey with the fans/heater off and windows closed Jessie mentions feeling something cold brush against her. I've felt similar myself at home, along with sounds from loud bangs to clicks which weren't present before. One of my brothers has seen him in a mirror. We've all witnessed candles flicker when we say his name or speak about someone within the family. It could be dismissed as a breeze passing through the candle but it doesn't happen any other time. For me he is communicating, and even if he isn't the children have comfort in feeling that he is still with us and watching over them. Instead of embracing Jessie's belief, Connor puts her down and uses science to explain the flicker. Does it really hurt for Jessie to have her own beliefs even if it doesn't conform to his own? This alienates Jessie and negatively impacts on her ability to open up to those up north.

The reality is that no-one can be definitively correct in knowing what happens after we have died until we endure the moment ourselves. Debating and criticising each other is pointless. A cynic won't change their mind and a believer won't be discouraged. Bullies though, hate people to have free will and think for themselves. Connor is a wonderful human being, I say with every bit of sarcasm.

My grandmother came through who sadly died when I was too young to remember her. There were personal references for my mum which validated to her that Bob was communicating with her. Things were relayed to my mum that only her mother would know. She was aware of a lovely gesture done after the funeral. Then she laid a bombshell on me.

"This one here can cope with a lot. He has strong shoulders. You can put everything on him when you feel down," My grandmother assured my mother. Bob pointed at me as the person to who she was referring.

I am strong-willed but even I have my breaking point. Recently life had been rather trying and difficult. To expect so much of me seemed rather foolhardy. I looked at my mum with amazement as if to say is she sure. I guess thinking back to everything I have been through and continue to endure I am rather strong. I don't let anything defeat me. Constantly fight on and persevere regardless of the difficulty.

On a different occasion a few months later my mum bumped into Sal, the psychic I had the reading with two years prior. She mentioned to mum that I will be in a relationship soon with a Jenny. She will come back into my life. Rather odd as a Jenny hasn't been in my life let alone come back. I was confused two years ago. To continue with the same name with such certainty was madness. The strange thing is my upcoming date is with a Jennifer. Could that be the Jenny? If so, I haven't known her prior so how could she be coming back?

More shocking revelations were revealed in conversation. Apparently, Connor and Casey are arguing. He desires a baby but Casey doesn't want any more kids. Didn't come as a surprise to me. I felt from the moment I heard of Connor that he would want a child of his own and that Casey would never have any more as she never intended to have the ones she already has. The shock was that they will have a baby together. My mind was blown. I know before Casey or even Connor. I never thought Casey would ever have more children. It's not in her to be a mother. She craves a carefree life without responsibilities. To reset time and endure another eighteen years of parenting was crazy. Time will tell whether this event transpires.

Casey doesn't cope well with pregnancy or raising children. Her depression and anxiety reached fever pitch. Connor would have to step up and be there by her side throughout all of the difficult moments. Could he sacrifice money and career to be there by her side? I doubt it. Most people wouldn't. I did. For a long time she needed me for everything and I never once failed her. I was reliable, dependable and absolutely dedicated to my family. Financially it was difficult but there are more important things in life than money.

I expect Connor to favour his own child when or if he/she arrives. He doesn't get on with Emma on any level and Jessie is becoming more fed up with his antics. Pushing Jessie away will only bring her closer into my care. I have no feelings good or bad about a potential baby for them. I'm only ever concerned about how things affect Jessie. Of course it would be of interest to her having another sister or a brother. Sal had stated there is a problem with the mothers genetics whereby there's too many issues with a boy. She can only have girls. This statement made her prophecy all the more real as she was spot on. It's absolutely an issue Casey has to contend.

There was something strange among the readings which I find curious. At no point has anyone mentioned me being an author. Books aren't mentioned at any stage within the readings. The most recent was only a swift conversation on passing rather than a full scheduled meeting. Still it would seem an obvious topic to acknowledge if they are seeing my future. Aside from Jessie, publishing my first book *A Father's Daughter* is my most significant accomplishment. Yet it doesn't even get a mention. That in itself does raise some scepticism, though so much has come true which can't simply be dismissed.

15

ROMANCE

For a single moment, the stars aligned creating an opportunity for a fairytale ending. The chance appeared to move my life romantically forward. A wonderful date ensued. I was shocked by her beauty and incredibly friendly persona. I probably talked too much. I was comfortable and not nervous in any way. Maybe I was too comfortable and let too much information role off of my tongue.

A topic I hate discussing more than any other is the circumstances surrounding my daughter. Dialogue becomes dark quickly without intention. The hate I have for all involved consumes me. Yet again Casey has ruined something in my life. She has a hold on me like no other. Not through love or kinship. The hold is control of my life regarding my daughter and the immense hate within me towards her. It can't be contained.

There could be many reasons why the date didn't go as planned. If it is due to the bitterness between parents, then I couldn't blame someone with many options to pursue a different course. I for one wouldn't want to be involved in this mess, but with my daughter at the centre, there is no alternative.

My date was warm, compassionate and understanding. A wonderful role model and example for Jessie to look up to. As a teacher, she has that aura of confidence and natural ability to listen intently. An opportunity missed which affected me for a while after. I had dared to dream for a moment of a positive future away from the mess and madness my life has to contend.

Our lives were different. She enjoys fine dining. A world away from what I am used to. But it is something I would learn to embrace and I'm sure it would be a nice and elegant change to my life. It's always nice to try new things and I want Jessie to grow up with that freedom to explore new places.

The search continues for my romantic partner and potential female role-model for Jessie. For now, I've decided not to continue looking. My heart is broken from Jessie's situation. It wouldn't be able to regularly withstand those romantic disappointments. We're fine on our own. Maybe for now that's how it needs to be until life brings us permanently together. In just over two years Jessie will have her say on where she wants to live. Her decision hasn't changed throughout this saga, so I'm preparing for the eventuality that she returns.

I had hoped to have a family situation with a partner ready for her to embrace, but it's looking more likely that it will have to wait until our hearts are restored and able to handle rejections. The support I have had has been wonderful from those close by and as far afield as Canada and Australia. I have received so many pearls of wisdom and encouragement to continue building on everything I have been doing. Eventually, life will hand Jessie and I that fairytale ending. I think maybe, for everything we have endured, it's something we both deserve.

16

INSPIRATION

The journey north for my weekend with Jessie at the beginning of November 2019 was horrendous. At the start of the trip, the estimated travel time was four hours, covering 250 miles. Mid-way, accidents and delays on the roads caused chaos and disruption. The estimate remained at four hours. It was as though my car was stuck on a gym treadmill working hard but making no progress getting to the destination.

After going off-route and driving different roads than usual, the estimated time reduced dramatically. The M1 and A50 were proving to be a nightmare, passing through smaller towns and avoiding the congestion helped wonders. I arrived at Jessie's school just ten minutes late. The alternative was around one and a half hours delay. She was engrossed talking to friends and teachers as I walked through the school corridors. As I approached closer, I could hear a short conversation.

"Mummy's here Jessie."

"No. No. No. My dad's coming to get me." Jessie pleaded

At that moment, I appeared around the corner and cuddled Jessie. The timing was surreal. I hadn't initially noticed the mention of Casey. Even after I hugged, I still hadn't caught sight of her. It was only as the teacher commented.

"That's some journey you do," she said with an astonished gaze.

"It's fine, I'm used to it," I responded unfazed.

Unbeknown to me while I was responding to the teacher, Casey beaconed Jessie for a cuddle. Later Jessie insisted that she didn't want to, but she had no choice. I only saw Casey when Jessie walked back to me. The glimpse of her was a blur as I had no interest. It was an arduous journey to make it to the school when I did. My concentration was on Jessie and getting her home. She did mention that Casey had rolled her eyes, visibly exasperated by my presence. Casey had arrived for a meeting with the head-teacher and expected Jessie to have left before her arrival.

Casey never informs me of school reports or appointments. Holding herself in regard as the only parent of importance. She always agrees with the teachers and makes sure to be on their right side by insisting that she will help Jessie at home with work; however, no help provided.

The journey home was perplexing—less than one mile from the M1 traffic ground to a halt. Being stuck so close to the junction was frustrating, especially as we had such a long journey ahead of us.

We arrived home later than expected but enjoyed ourselves along the way as we stopped in services for McDonald's and then further on to another for a hot drink. My mind and body were exhausted. The delays and stress of the journey had taken everything out of me. I usually allow Jessie to stay up late as our time together is so limited. On this occasion, I needed to rest and recover sooner than usual.

When we awoke the following day, I thought it would be a fun idea to take Jessie to the same location where I had had my recent date. The hot chocolate was amazing, and I wanted Jessie to experience it along with seeing for herself where I had been. She was excited and eager, more so for the hot chocolate than anything else. It comes with a Flake chocolate bar and tiny biscuit.

Parking the car across the road from the beach was eventful. Walking down the street in the direction of the sea caused winds to hit us full force. Jessie and I were struggling to contend with the ferocity. I couldn't help myself. Suddenly I over-reacted, throwing myself into the wall spinning uncontrollably as the winds lashed into us. Jessie was in hysterics laughing and joining in my games. Cars slowed as they passed by. I'm sure it was a sight to behold and a talking point for many. Jessie and I lost in a bubble of fun.

17

FRUSTRATION

As the week progressed, Jessie communicated less frequent. Days went by without any engagement. I knew that this was Casey's biding but chose not to pursue the matter. I instead reduced my text message output and waited on Jessie to get in touch with me. Sometimes our conversations and messages flow with charisma, banter and whimsical gusto. Other moments it's more strained and less expansive. None more evident than during phone calls.

By the end of the first week of November 2019, Jessie hadn't been her usual vibrant self. I had been looking forward to our telephone call. We only get the one call a week, so I like to make it count. There was much to discuss, many stories to tell, and laughs to share. Then there are the potential activities Jessie has partaken during the Halloween and Guy Fawkes week. I was eager to hear of the fun she may have enjoyed, and fireworks witnessed. That was the plan at least. We didn't get that far or anywhere of significance.

The phone call was to take place on Friday evening. She was slightly late calling and hadn't responded to my previous message sent a few hours prior. I had just trimmed my hair and ready to get in the bath when the phone rang. It was a surprise as the muted silence all day felt eerily similar to the moment of Jessie's abduction. There was an intense feeling of De-Ja-Vu as though our contact was about to be disrupted. It was a relief to hear the phone ring. I had contemplated contacting my solicitors to garner the next move should the call not happen. Since Court concluded and legal assistance finished, I have remained in contact with my solicitors on a personal level. We are all human and endured a monumental event together. I provided them with copies of *A Father's Daughter*. It was the least I could do, considering everything they have done for me.

The call connected. Jessie was lethargic. Polite but not in the mood to talk. Sometimes she can be like that. Most of the time, it's due to Casey. That's why my frustrations surface. I'm not offended by Jessie. If she's happy, I'm delighted. I just know what Casey's game is, and what she tries to accomplish. Gets her busy for that one moment when our phone call is due. Shortly after disbands and leaves Jessie lonely and isolated as they withdraw to their humdrum life. Then Jessie has the realisation that she could now do with a fun conversation with her father. Instead, it's wasted on a moment in the middle of doing something. In this case, Casey was selecting new beds for Jessie and Emma. Of course, Jessie would want to be involved in the selection process. Surely it could've waited or been done before the call.

"Hello," I greeted in a silly voice.

"Hi," Jessie responded quietly.

"What you been up to?"

"I'm with mummy and Emma choosing high beds."

"Why would you want to be near the ceiling?"

"It's fun,"

"So what you been up to?"

"Nothing."

"Didn't see the fireworks?"

"Oh, yeah, I did see them."

Emma and Casey surrounded Jessie. Not a positive place for us to be in, as she can't freely talk, and they are distracting. In my opinion - on purpose.

"I have a class assembly Thursday."

"What do you mean assembly? A performance?"

"Yeah, its to do with Greek gods."

"I won't get to see that."

"No."

"You may as well be on the moon, as your so far away."

"The moon," Jessie repeated laughing.

"You okay? you haven't been talking much."

"Phone calls are boring."

"Oh. okay, shall we just end the call."

"No. It's fine."

"No point talking if you don't want to."

"I want to."

We then continued talking a little longer, but it wasn't going anywhere, and I didn't feel the urge to open up about my week while Jessie is in the presence of others. I had rushed from the gym to get home, charge my phone and get ready for our call. This one sadly was a waste of time. The call lasted five minutes. Usually, it's around half-hour. I could've talked for hours but didn't see the point if Jessie isn't in the mood.

Everything is frustrating. I don't hear directly from Casey or the school regarding Jessie's activities or progress. When we were together Casey, and I agreed if we ever separate we would remain amicable and always put the children first. It would seem that she was just copying me at the time. The next step would be to receive regular updates from the school on Jessie's progress from reports, activities and appointments. Casey had recently attended a meeting with the head-teacher. I only know this as I was collecting Jessie from school while Casey was waiting in the reception area. At no point has she or the school informed me of the appointment, the reason for or the outcome of the meeting. If Casey has overexerted her authority and placed me into a less significant role within the school, then I will find out. A polite request to the school was submitted. If there are obstructions, then I will instruct solicitors to communicate with the school to resolve the situation and keep on file any issues reported.

It would have been nice if Casey could give me updates herself, but she has never bothered to date, and our relationship is at an all-time low.

18

INTERFERANCE

Bless Casey; she doesn't like to go unnoticed. I don't look in her direction or walk over during the return handover of Jessie. We say our goodbyes with a heartfelt cuddle. Jessie always pleads to remain with me, but I insist she must return and reassure her that I will be back again soon. She leaves the car and walks the few short steps back into her mothers care. I then drive off swiftly to get as far away from Casey as I can.

I had blocked her phone number for a good month or so. The constant manipulation of my words and misinformation reached a point within me of ceasing communication. It's just not productive, and I lose a bit of my soul with every engagement.

My email to the school for reports and information received a polite reply from the headteacher. She explained that they remain impartial to family situations but will keep me informed of Jessie's development along with sending her recent school report. There was also an upcoming parents evening I could attend separately to Casey. It felt nice to finally have insight into Jessie's schooling aside from just collecting her from class once fortnightly.

I relayed to Jessie via Whats App

Collecting you from school Friday. Spoke to the headteacher. You and I have a meeting with your teacher so you can show me your work and find out how you're doing. Your headteacher told me you've been wonderful :)

To my surprise on the same day that I received Jessie's school report in the post, Casey had also sent a letter. She wants to try and find a way for us to be amicable and communicate directly each week and not through Jessie. In all honesty, I don't think I could engage with her that frequent. It would drive me to madness. She said all the right things in many aspects on paper, which was her only goal. Create a well-worded piece of paper for evidence to show that she is trying to work with me on Jessie's welfare. At no point prior has she ever kept me updated on Jessie's schooling. Now that she knows I will have an insight she wants to communicate. More like she wants to know what I've been told by the school. I'm not a fool.

At the end of her letter, Casey had accused me of posting inappropriate content on my social media channels. She deemed it to be harassment. If it continues, Casey will report me to CAFCASS and the police. It was clear that she didn't want me promoting my books and control my life. At no point have I ever revealed her real identity or whereabouts. I don't tag or even try and engage with her or anyone associated.

In contrast, she stalks my social media to complain about posts which may offend her. There's nothing said that I would feel embarrassed by or regret. My main concern is why go out of the way to look for me and get offended. Move on in life and be blissfully unaware. She upsets herself and behaves like a victim. Her behaviour is embarrassing.

I sent a response via Whats App to Casey. It wasn't a friendly response, but she had had her say in the letter. Now it's my turn to say what I feel. It can't always be one-way traffic, though if she could have it her way it certainly would be her speak, I listen.

I just received your letter. I would love to see the posts where I refer to you by name. I would suggest you stop stalking me online. I don't search for you or anyone associated. The order about posts was during court proceedings which have concluded. I've always been open to dialogue but grew tired of the manipulative twist on my words. You had Jessie have a counsellor and question whether she was a good girl yet the school have told me how wonderful she is. I believe she does suffer emotional abuse in your care. I continue to make notes. I'm collecting Jessie from school Friday as I have a meeting with the teacher shortly after. If we can be cordial, then I am open to keeping messages open. I will, of course, forward your letter to my solicitors for filling.

Immediately after sending the message, I attached a copy of the letter and copied my response to an email which was sent directly to my solicitors. It was evident to me that Casey is starting preparation to gather evidence to use in Court, which she knows is inevitable as I will be applying to the Court when Jessie is of a mature age. I am sure Casey wants me to react sooner so that she can disrupt our contact, but

I won't take the bait. I will apply precisely when I mean to (a Lord of the Rings reference).

One would think that having received a response to her letter that Casey would be eager to engage in communication, considering that's what she indicated within her correspondence. Sadly, no. It was all for a show to have on that piece of paper. I expected no less. I can see through everything Casey does. It doesn't take a professor to see what's coming and why.

Within Jessie's school report was a reference to our weekends and holidays which Jessie regularly speaks positively about in class. By all accounts, the entire school knows when I'm arriving to collect her. Jessie is proud of my efforts and loves our time together, as do I.

To my surprise, the following day, Casey responded to my message reaffirming the need for us to communicate when needed regarding Jessie's welfare. If I've learnt anything from the past, it is never to trust her; there are always ulterior motives. Nothing is ever how it seems, but I will at least give her the benefit of the doubt. It would be helpful for everyone to stop the bickering.

19

SCHOOL

Meeting Jessie's school teacher was a great source of enjoyment for me. Before the upheaval in our lives, I had been a regular at her school. Watching performances and attending parent's evenings. Now, finally, I could take part in something most parents take for granted. Get to see how Jessie is doing at school. Visit her classroom and see the world she lives daily.

The time with her teacher was insightful and lighthearted. We shared laughs and some life stories. It was a good experience which I wanted to cherish. The journey to the school was exhausting. Sleep was difficult the night prior. My eyes were strained and sore with each passing mile on the trip north. Arrived exhausted by the time I collected Jessie. However, I was able to communicate effectively with a good conversation, trying to read Jessie's workbooks became problematic. I attempted one page five times but had to admit defeat.

"I can't seem to take in the pages. The journey has been long; I'm rather tired. Sorry"

"That's fine. Feel free to speak to me whenever you collect Jessie from school if you have any questions."

"The main thing I wanted to know is how she gets on in class, and what I should be helping her with?"

"She is wonderful, laughs a lot, but does her work. She's very involved with class activities and popular with the class."

"How about reading, writing and maths?"

"She excels at maths."

"Bit of a brainiac like me. I like maths as it's a challenge and like a puzzle."

"I like maths too."

"Maths is easy," Jessie interrupted.

"Ooh. You know what that means don't you? Say you're great, then we'll expect perfection. Boom, under pressure now," I said with a wink.

"No." Jessie pleaded.

"What does she struggle with the most? She finds some words hard to read, such as the Shakespeare book. I did tell her if it's someone's name just pronounce how you think it should be read, but be confident and consistent. Then no-one will question your delivery."

"That's the best way. She needs to practise her spellings and handwriting, though it is improving. She was awarded a pen," The teacher said with a smile.

Jessie raised a smile of her own in response.

"Her mum was planning to come up the school and demand she has a pen, but I told Jessie it's better to earn it. She'll get one when she's ready, and it would mean so much more than just being given it."

Jessie and her teacher both smiled. It was, of course, much more rewarding and the right behavioural trait to learn.

I had taken up more of the teachers time than either of us had planned. We all enjoyed the time together. It was an open and honest discussion. At one point during the meeting, Jessie leant over to me, giving me a kiss and a cuddle. The teacher's eyes lit up as she had witnessed and heard of the long journey's I endure and now she was witnessing us together for the first time. There could be no denying our bond.

The journey home was the most exhausting I have ever endured. The lack of sleep caused a bloodshot blot on my right eye due to the constant strain from driving. A latte purchased on the way north hadn't helped much, if at all. On the journey South with Jessie, we stopped off at the services as usual. I bought her a keyring with the letter of her name which she had desired for a few weeks.

Jessie had her typical choice Chicken Nugget Happy Meal from McDonald's. She has branched out in rotating her drink options. For a long time, the only choice was Chocolate Milkshake or water. Now she also likes Oasis which to her delight isn't fizzy. I always ask if she wants the more substantial Chicken Nugget Meal. Depends on her appetite which meal she chooses. Either way, it's Chicken Nuggets which drives me crazy. I could hardly complain, though, seeing as I always select a Burger. Sometimes vary the choice but still a Burger. The usual Coca-Cola option was wasted on me as I needed caffeine. I opted for the Christmas exclusive Millionaire's Latte, which had cream and sauce poured on top. At the time I enjoyed the drink. I would later get another which wasn't as memorable. Rather sickly in-fact.

Jessie had been nodding off tired as we neared our destination home. I couldn't wait to finally rest my eyes and get out of the tin box I had lost an entire day within. She awoke in plenty of time as we got nearer. I was surprised upon returning home. Jessie had sprung to life with no regard for the late arrival. I, on the other hand, was tired and exhausted. I did allow for her to watch a single episode of a TV show until I couldn't cope any longer. She too was tired but was trying her best to fight it. It didn't take her long to fall asleep in bed.

We awoke to a variety of song requests from Alexa on the Echo Dot audio device. Recent country music from my play-list, Ariana Grande and older tracks such as Agadoo, Backstreet Boys and anything random I could recollect. I like Jessie to hear music beyond the current charts. Build up a music knowledge of songs from the past. On our journey the previous day, I introduced her to Queen, Elton John and Whitney Houston. Some of the most decorated artists and bands ever. Almost a sin not to hear and know their songs. She knew some songs and sang along to the choruses.

I had planned to take Jessie for a hot chocolate; however the venue we were heading appeared full with cars

114

overspilling onto the side streets outside of the car park. We headed into town instead so we could browse shops. She doesn't get to visit shops with her mother, so while we both like to spend time at home together and get cosy, I don't want her to grow up thinking the world is just indoors. So we venture out to create memories and be part of the world. She cost me considerable money on this trip but always worth it. I needed inspiration for Christmas, and she didn't disappoint. A giant cute black dog teddy with neon blue eyes had her smitten. The shock on her face when I said, "I'll get it," was priceless. She hadn't expected me to say yes with finances a little tighter than I had hoped.

"For Christmas though. If I give you everything, we're going to have problems later," I explained.

"Okay." Jessie acknowledged.

The teddy had been the last one available on the shelf. I didn't want Jessie to hope for it and then be disappointed. It gave her something to look forward to and be excited. The reality is she doesn't have a big Christmas list this year. She already has most things she would want. I was using this trip as inspiration for Christmas while also aware that I may either forget later or struggle to get the items so was trying my best to keep up and get now.

This year Jessie will be spending Christmas Day with her mother. I won't have her home until Boxing Day. Presents wise I feel this year is more about what her mother gets her and my turn is next year although of course, I want to get her everything I can. The reality though is that Jessie simply isn't home long enough at any moment to play and enjoy presents once they're opened. We often struggle to find time to watch a movie together, let alone play with toys. The distance affects us both in so many ways. Witnessing Jessie clinging desperately to the time we have together is always heartbreaking.

The shopping spree continued with a Harry Potter drinking bottle and pink flask for school. I was at odds trying to understand the need for both.

"I need a flask for my drinks at school. I asked mummy she won't get it." Jessie explained.

"Do you need both though?"

Jessie looked worried. Unsure which one to dismiss.

"Okay. I'll just get both as long as your going to use them. You can have the flask now and take that back with you to mummies. The Harry Potter bottle will be Christmas."

"YES," Jessie said, visibly overjoyed.

She was thrilled when I also bought her a new drawing pad and colouring pencils. Sometimes it's the most simple things which give the most pleasure. I love Jessie's creativity and will always embrace and encourage her.

Then she whisked me over to the Christmas sweet isle. I had to show restraint. If she had her way, we'd be getting everything in the shop. Chocolate could wait as we have snacks at home. I did, however, get my mum a large tube of Jaffa Cakes. Not suitable for one's health, but she loves them. Should tide her over for a while.

On our way to the next shopping experience, we stopped into the cinema. I wanted to get a leaflet to find out what movies are coming out soon. Jessie then wanted to watch a film, but the cinema was too busy, and there was nothing worth watching. Soon though there will be many movies releasing which we could watch. Jessie was pleading, but I had to balance money and our time. We have a family party in the evening which she wants to attend. Today wasn't the time for the cinema.

A stage and large screen appeared at the top end of the high street. Jessie and I watched and enjoyed the dancers and singers. The local college performed an excellent performance of a song from the movie *The Greatest Showman*. Always awe-inspiring watching talent on stage. We moved on to WH Smith. Jessie loves the shop as it has pens, pencil cases, books and everything in between. I bought her the newly released *Diary of a Wimpy Kid: Wrecking Ball* which came with a free book. A nice bonus.

After a two hour excursion into town, we made our way home. I initially stopped at The Harvester restaurant to take Jessie for a meal, but she just wanted to be home instead. I then detoured to the shop instead and we headed back. Jessie and I watched the Disney movie The Nutcracker which we both enjoyed.

At 6.30 pm we drove 40 miles to Harlow, Essex. A journey I wasn't excited to make considering the vast distance covered the previous day and again tomorrow. Plus there's the travel home after the party. So much driving in a short space of time. Somewhat maddening in all honesty, though it's nice to have the family together and Jessie was eager. I wouldn't be able to forgive myself if I didn't do my best to get her there to wish her cousins a Happy Birthday. For her it was a great success. She loved spending time with everyone especially one cousin she has no memory of seeing before. Our family is large and spread out. The distance Jessie resides doesn't make it any easier. I always anticipated that Skyla and Jessie would get on wonderfully; they even added each other to the video game Roblox. Oakley's arrival had the group together. I gave them plenty of time although Jessie had lost track pleading with me for longer when I declared that we are leaving. 10.20 pm was late enough considering the journey back and extensive travel the following day. She was disappointed, but I was firm, not a moment for negotiating. Even another five minutes wasn't going to happen. We all know that five minutes ends up being thirty or more as time gets away from everyone.

She was okay on the journey home. We had a late McDonalds. It wasn't ideal to have the same meal on consecutive days but options at this time of night were scarce. Better than nothing. Couldn't have her go to bed hungry.

"I only want a drink. I'm so thirsty," Jessie explained.

"I'll get you a meal."

"I don't think I could eat it. I'm just thirsty."

"If you don't eat it, I will, but at least it's there if you change your mind."

Thankfully Jessie's appetite did arrive once we got home. She devoured her food without much effort. More hungry than she even realised. A long day for us both, but eventful and more memories created. A good weekend together.

The journey to return Jessie was a nightmare. Darkness arrives earlier than usual, and the weather changes along the route are remarkably varied. One moment visibility is clear, the next there's a torrential downpour with water spray causing driving conditions to be severe. Visibility diminished on fast treacherous roads. Accidents extend the travel time along the way. Jessie was doing her best to keep her mother updated. We had a pit-stop at the services on-route for a meal, drink and toilet break.

We arrived just in time to witness Casey and Connor walking up. I try my best to keep away from them, as my disgust runs deep. On this occasion, I had no choice but to get out of the car as Jessie had bags in the boot. As Jessie was leaving the car and walking to me, I could hear a loud booming voice behind me at a distance.

"Hello. Are you okay?"

I rolled my eyes, keeping my back to them as I helped zip Jessie's coat. It amazes me that he has to make himself heard. I have no time for him at all. Saying anything will only make Jessie uncomfortable, so I just leave him to be him but give no attention.

"Need help with any bags?" Connor asked.

I looked in his direction, "No. She's fine."

If he had started with that question, I would give him props for being polite and asking to be of help. The loud introduction while Jessie and I were trying to say our goodbyes lost him any goodwill from me. I can see through him, and I don't do two-faced niceties. If I don't like someone, they will know. There is no grey area. My mum was in attendance. She too wasn't impressed with his interruption but like me felt he sounded polite and friendly enough after. I have no interest in playing games though and don't trust him or Casey.

20

EXASPERATED

Within a day or two of a compromise agreement between Casey and I, there was cause for concern. Jessie confirmed that she is affected by others during our telephone calls. Her mother likes to listen in to our conversation and Connor doesn't allow her to talk in peace and comfort. Instead, he antagonises by waving and condescendingly saying *love you* while we are speaking. He doesn't seem to cope without attention. Jealousy consumes his behaviour. By now, he should be used to the bond Jessie, and I share. It's not going to go away, and anything he does isn't going to get in the way of that bond. A moron trying to be whimsical and noticed, instead he was coming across as pathetic and desperate.

When Jessie spoke to me about my book, *A Father's Daughter*, I was deeply alarmed. I don't go into detail about the book, nor do I read her the story. I had sent her a photo of the book within a Whats App message. Casey noticed and took her desperation to new deplorable lengths. In her attempts to blame me for traumatising and causing distress,

121

she forced Jessie to read the cover in full and mentioned to her the contents of the book. Her behaviour disgusts me and shows no sign of abating. Her offers of a positive resolution and parties to unite are just words on a page and a text. Her behaviour is manipulative and controlling.

"Are you okay with what's written?" Casey asked Jessie as she read the entire front cover. Including the subtitle, *A Daughters Abduction Leaves A Father FIGHTING FOR JUSTICE!*

"Yeah," Jessie responded.

"Really?"

"Yeah."

Casey was surprised by Jessie's comfort with the story title. Probably expecting her to be defensive of her mother, but like me, she isn't impressed with Casey's behaviour. She still mentions to this day "We were only supposed to go to the dentist." A reference to the moment she was abducted from school.

"I know that there will be a third book," Casey said.

Jessie shrugged her shoulders. She was choosing not to acknowledge her mother's remarks. Jessie was aware that I had decided to write the books as a trilogy with the third book releasing after she returns home to live with me. Both of us are waiting for her to reach the age of twelve years old. We were failed by the Court before but looking forward to the moment she can decide for herself where she resides. Casey knows this too. It was evident that she had been looking through my social media posts. Obsessive and something of a stalker. The obsession of me is strange. Casey left me, yet continues to check on me regularly.

Throughout the weekend Casey had been messaging Jessie with updates of her new bed being built. I was amazed that it took three days to assemble. Surely there isn't any furniture requiring that amount of time to piece together. Connor sent photos of himself. Every day he tries to be more like me. My goofy and silliness doesn't come across on paper, but I'm often compared to Mr Bean and Jim Carrey. Spontaneously goofy and silly. Connor tries, but he isn't original.

For a moment picture me as Jim Carrey in the movie Liar Liar. Connor is the mother's new boyfriend whom embracingly tries to do the claw. That's where the similarities end. I am always there for Jessie, never letting her down, unlike the lawyer character portrayed in the movie. Connor is disruptive and manipulative, which isn't at all like the boyfriend in the film.

The lives in the movie were dysfunctional due to Jim Carrey's characters irregular contact with his son. Our lives are dysfunctional by the mother and boyfriends behaviour and disruption. Roles reversed as the mother in the movie was inspiring with the commitment to her son.

The movie is an excellent example of our life. The Court's decision favoured the unfit mother over a loving and adoring father. Justice isn't always fair.

Connor explained to Jessie that he suffers from bullying online. People have been saying nasty things about him. Jessie smiled at me as she shared this memory.

"Ah. That's not nice," Jessie responded to Connor's claims of being a victim with a sly smile.

He gazed at her with a look of certainty that she knew as to what he was alluding. It's Jessie's opinion that he was referencing my social media outbursts when I posted exerts from chapters of this book onto Facebook and Twitter. If he didn't behave like a Neanderthal, then I wouldn't have bad words to say about him, but much like Casey, he is now trying to play the victim. I can't say I regret anything I have ever said or done. If I've reacted or posted something, then there would be a reason for that action.

21

INJUSTICE

The response on social media to everything endured was overwhelming. Everyone could see through Connor's attention seeking behaviour and Casey's disruption. They encouraged me to persist with our phone calls. The distractions had me wondering whether it's worth Jessie having the calls. It wasn't something I was looking to alter any time soon but was a question in my mind as to what is in her best interests. The consensus was to keep being the adult and role-model for Jessie, so that she has a barometer on what life should be like as opposed to the behaviour exerted of those in her life where she resides.

I have a friend in the same situation. Fortunately, his daughter isn't swayed by her mother's and step-father's corrosive behavior.

That sort of behavior is unlikely to change my friend. Some people simply do not have the maturity.

She'll remember you called her every week regardless of how stupid they were ♥

125

You keep on calling her and show her what respect and true love is, in time she will see and appreciate all the moments you were with her.

Be her steady guidestar to how adults should nurture.

Absolutely worth it! Why give them any power in the situation! You and your daughter, that's what you focus on. She'll always remember the time you gave her & will love you always for it! MHO Hugs 😊

So annoying. I have a similar thing-whenever I call my best friend her husband attention seeks the whole time. These people are needy and insecure. Can't have someone's attention off them for half an hour.

Hard to be the adult when others act so childish.

Yes. Beat them, no matter how long it takes. Your daughter will treasure the phone calls with you, and forget the stupid behavior in the background.

Yes, be the adult in her life. She will remember.

Ughhhhhhhhh-sorry you have to go through crap like that! I can relate! Stay strong! (I've wondered myself stuff like this, and I just try to balance it as best I can) 😜

Yep. She will remember your efforts and failures. Persevere, man. Make her know she is always your first choice.

126

A HEARTBROKEN DAUGHTER

A lady from Canada had taken incredible exception to Casey. The behaviour had hit a nerve within her. I couldn't bare to tell her of the outcome as she was already getting fired up. It was her opinion that Casey should have visitation access rescinded with no access to Jessie. Little did she know that Jessie currently resides in her mothers care. She did eventually figure it out from a later post I had made about the long journeys endured.

You have got to be kidding me?

You couldn't make it up. The injustice is ridiculous. I bet she still doesn't understand why I will never like her.

I wouldn't either. Just the thought of her harming her child like she is makes me sick! That woman needs to be locked up! I don't know you or your daughter but I am angry. There is no justice to allow that to happen. The courts are not looking out for that little girl at all!

Every single court hearing the mother delayed proceedings by trying to make it all about her rather than our daughter. Twice our contact was suspended by her false claims. I appealed the decisions, and went for cross examinations, miraculously on the day she's fine with contact but only after we had suffered a month of separation the first time and three months the second. I can't ever tolerate or trust her. Too vindictive and manipulative. By the end it was evident the judge wanted to order her home with me but the child case worker had been swayed by the Mother's lies. Had he chosen me she could've appealed which would be more disruption for Jessie.

That is absurd! I think the child case workers don't always listen to what is being said. Did they do a mental evaluation on the mother? She needs one now! I hope your daughter sees her, (I can't even use the word mother, I can't even capitalize that word for her) for what she is . In time, I am sure your daughter will want nothing to do with her. She is a monster in disguise! It just infuriates me!!! For her to use that child, she is no mother. There was no justice in this case. You are a great Dad to fight for that precious angel!

Thank you. I don't like speaking negatively of the mother but I no longer have anything nice to say about her. Doesn't inform me of school performances. When I enquired about sports day she tried to say it was a different day so I miss it. For my own sanity, I try not to communicate with her very often. More distance between us the better. I'm confident my daughter will be home in just over 2 years. She has her heart set on it, and I will be more than ready to fight for her once again.

That will be a blessed day for both of you. Can you get the schools, or her activities to send you messages as well so you know what she is doing? I can speak negatively because I think she is lower than shit for what she is doing to that child! Sorry, I am opinionated and I have a strong dislike for people who treat children poorly.

For strangers to have strong views on the injustice, serious questions are raised about the UK Family Court's process and decision making. The judgement didn't make any sense when it was handed down and declared. To this day I'm still shocked at the outcome.

How can someone lie throughout, commit perjury, slander, abduction and then be victorious and to add further insult not have to travel? Declaring financial hardship while hiding a relationship which I had made the Court aware of multiple times. Then when proceedings concluded he swiftly moved into her new place of residence. It's disgusting on so many levels, yet I am expected to make peace and get along with these people who continue to cause difficulties and problems.

22

ALONE

Early December 2019, Jessie shared an alarming observation with me.

"Mummies and Connor's families don't like me," Jessie said as she held her head low and sad.

"I'm sure they do like you. Your fun to be around."

"No. I know they don't."

"Well, don't let it bother you. You have our family, and we adore you."

"I know, but it does make me sad. I don't like people not liking me."

"I'm sure it's just because of how you are with me, rather than anything about you.

"Maybe. But I want them to like me."

"Don't waste your energy on people that don't deserve you. Make the most of people that show they care." I said, trying my best to give her a positive mindset.

Jessie's sadness weighed on her mind long after our conversation. We are so similar in so many ways, but this is one part of our personalities where we differ. I don't waste my time on negative people, nor do I allow others opinions to affect me. I couldn't care less who likes and doesn't like me. I am happy in myself to know my qualities. However, I didn't want to force my beliefs onto Jessie. If it affects her and makes her sad, then that's her right to feel that way.

Hopefully, in time she will make peace with the fact that you can't make everyone like you. People have their agendas. In this case, Connor's parents will prioritise him, maybe Jessie not getting on with him at times rubs them the wrong way. Likewise, Jessie favouring me and desiring to leave her mother will feel like a betrayal to her family. They should be grown up enough not to take it personally or cause such distress to a minor, but that's not their style. Bullies don't conform to morals. Desiring their attention makes no sense to me, but in any case, she shouldn't have to beg.

23

STALKING

For as long as I can remember, my social media profiles have been monitored and stalked obsessively by undesirables. Casey and her entourage take an alarming interest in every aspect of my life. One would think that she has the life of her dreams; after all, she got what she wanted. The continuing curiosity of me is strange and intrusive. I can't say anything or interact with people without any of them taking notes, then passing onto Casey which she often uses in unsuitable conversations with Jessie. Our child shouldn't have to bear the burden of her mother's insecurities and anxiety. Who cares what I say? For all I know aside from what Casey says to Jessie, I don't know what she tells other people. I don't search for her and have zero interest.

Facebook is within easy reach of Casey and her family. It's a platform which they comfortably understand. Twitter, on the other hand, is alien to them. Complicated and too much of a learning curve even for the interest in me. I reluctantly closed my Facebook author page, against the advice of many. I saw no other way to get the people I want out of my life away from me, at the least not give them such insights into my life. They took it away from me, another something lost. For my sanity, it was the best decision I could make in the circumstances.

People have suggested Casey's behaviour probably stems from her *still* having feelings for me. She can't let go of the past and move on. If so, Casey has a funny way of showing it by taking everything I hold dear away from me and making life a misery. Such a lovely person. Now she is someone else's problem. I've taken steps to reduce her activity in my life and feel better for it.

A negative review appeared on the UK Amazon store page of *A Father's Daughter*. I expect the same for this book too. I know Casey's behaviour and her mothers. I have nothing against honest reviews, but this one stood out to me immediately. I was ninety-nine per cent sure it was Casey's mother. She reminds me of Annie from Stephen King's *Misery* novel. A deranged and crazy obsessed woman. She is the epitome of evil — cunning, deceptive and manipulative. From here on out I will refer to her by a nickname as *Annie*. She edits the review randomly; you may see a different edition of it from time to time. Within the review, there is mention of *my* poor grammar. A blatant attempt to try and lower my self-esteem, sadly for her it did not work. The irony though is that her grammar was awful. The review garnered more interest in my book, which increased sales. Rather than hinder, she unwittingly assisted in promoting *A Father's Daughter*. Good karma for me.

I use my real name and face on my book and throughout social media. Annie hides behind the username *Amazon Customer* and no identifying characteristics. She hides in the shadows, watching my every move while using her user review as an outlet to communicate. Sadly for her, I no longer look as I have more meaningful and exciting things to occupy my mind.

There were specific sections of the review which gave it away for me. It should be noted that a negative review also appeared on the Audible product page for the audiobook within minutes of publishing. There wasn't enough time for someone to listen to more than the first chapter. Not suspicious at all. To catch Annie out, I sent Casey a text message mentioning that I know her mother left a review. I did this on purpose. If it were her, then she wouldn't take kindly to me not being bothered. There would be a reaction, and low and behold, she reacted.

I know you have people watching my every move online. I don't care and do what I do with no thought about them. I'm pretty sure your mum left me a lovely book review, wasn't obvious at all and again I don't care. There will always be haters. What I will say is at no point have I ever revealed your name, location or even what you look like, so who cares what I talk about. You could be on Mars for all anyone knows. Just saying it this once. It is hardly bullying when no one knows who you are.

Within a few hours, the review was edited, which contained details only Casey could have known. I didn't mention any of this on social media prior, but you bet your cotton socks I did share it with everyone after. People were shocked that Annie would stoop so low, not just in stalking which they found alarming but also leaving a vengeful review which bordered on harassment and potential lawsuit territory for slander. In my books everybody's names are protected. They have no reason to read my book or seek out what I am doing in my life, but they can't help themselves. I personally think that it eats them up inside knowing that the world doesn't believe their lies, so they try twisting, and twisting to sway people but just come across more malevolent. It's predictable and immature. I leave them to live in envy. I move forward with my life accomplishing life goals and have the adjuration of my daughter. I couldn't ask for more than that. How they decide to behave and live their lives is up to them. What I will say is that jealousy is neither flattering nor appealing.

24

TRAVEL

Age catches up with everyone eventually. No different for me; however, I am feeling it with each passing month. The journey's north can be excruciating on the mind and body. Restless nights before a long trip render a routine trip treacherous. One incident required me to pull over on the drive south after collecting Jessie. We waited outside services in the car as I rested and got a much-needed nap. My eyes burned like acid, head struggled to compute the world around us, and the body was feeling an ache never endured before.

For the past few months, well since I cared to notice, my eyes have suffered severely from the strain of staring at the roads for an entire day. The travel is direct from one motorway to the next, fast with no room for error or distraction. Taking a stroll at slower speeds would make the journey longer than it already is, and more sufferable. As it is, I have to monitor my eye. If it worsens, then our plans together could be in tatters. A blood vessel bursts resulting in a red blot to appear around the iris. It is often taking a week to disappear. How much strain can an eye endure? I have no idea, and I am worried to find out. My mum suggested the need to be careful as a blood clot could form. Others have encouraged me to seek medical advice from a doctor. For now, I endure, fighting on through the trauma to my body.

The travel we endure is not a short stroll past a few roads. It's an expedition across the entire country of England, and then a swift turn back home immediately after. One stretch is more than enough for one day, but I have no choice but to endure two. Over an entire weekend four sets of 250-miles. The costs are nothing to be sniffed at either. Two hundred pounds covers a weekend contact for fuel, meals and snacks. After all, I'm driving for an entire day from morning through to the night. The body needs fuelling just as much as the car.

Often when I arrive home, I am shocked to see my skin pale as a ghoulish tone replaces the natural pigmentation. The travel takes a toll on my body. I appear sheepish, nothing like the clean-cut, well-dressed man that started the journey. At the back of my mind, it is a worry. I can never spend too long dwelling, but those moments when I do return are shocking. If most people were to see me in those moments, they would consider me ill. For all, I know, maybe I am. Maybe each journey takes something out of me. Perhaps I am bound to this curse of an appearance. Jessie never notices as the transition is gradual during the travel. The same as someone living with a child, never seeing them grow. When I stop to visit my mum at the end of the journey, she always notes, "You look ill."

I am tired, but shrug it off as nothing more than exhaustion. Being constantly reminded at the end of every trip that I look awful is not the most pleasant experience. I do not suffer vanity, but I would not have thought that anyone could take a positive from a negative perception.

I will admit, sometimes I do not want to travel. The thought of getting in the car and starting the journey can be an effort in itself. I feel exhausted, just thinking about it, let alone physically driving. The only thing that gets me through is Jessie. When I think of her, an immense drive builds in me that allows me to take on the world and move mountains. That energy dissipates when it is time to return her. There is no motivation to travel an entire day against the tides of traffic to a place she does not want to go. She wants to stay with me. I can barely recollect a moment when she does not want to stay. The odd moment when there is a school event is the only time she has spoken positively of returning. Never has it been to be with her mother or sister. Casey really should be collecting her on the Sundays. The burden should not fall solely onto me. I think any other judge would have ordered her to travel for that journey at least. It's not only a financial burden but physically and mentally draining. An incredible weight is on my shoulders to never miss a trip. Surely if Jessie is so anxious to see me, then she should be with me.

Connor's behaviour is off and on. He can frighten Jessie, yet she is more open to seeing him than her natural family.

It should be for Casey to come and collect her from me as it is for most estranged couples with children. It is entirely unfair to put the burden of contact onto my shoulders alone. I should not bear the brunt of her decision to reside at the opposite end of the country. Playing the victim is farcical, and no one is buying it. She continues to play that card to appear innocent and blameless.

Jessie understands the travel difficulty. She had mentioned in January 2020 a few weeks after Christmas how unfair it is that we don't get to spend her birthday together.

"Why don't we get to spend my birthday together?" Jessie asked.

"Well. The court order does say that mummy and I are both allowed equal time with you, but, it's so far. I can't afford to travel for a few hours together when it's our weekend only a few days before or after. We can celebrate then."

Jessie nodded, understanding the predicament, "I wouldn't want to travel on my birthday."

She was a bit confused. It would not have been her travelling but me. If only she resided nearby like most families who have encountered a separation. Casey's decision to relocate so far causes more suffering than she would care to consider. I don't know if she has ever taken a step back to think of the impact her decisions have on those around her. It often plays on my mind that when Jessie is sad or had a bad day, especially as she grows and matures that she can not merely visit and have a hot chocolate while talking together. A simple gesture that most probably take for granted. For us, it is a fantasy. A dream. Nothing more than fiction. The distance between us makes it impossible. Her childhood is disappearing in front of my eyes, and Jessie has noticed it too.

25

MEDIUM

The man or woman who insists there are no ghosts is only ignoring the whispers of his or her own heart, and how cruel that seems to me.

- Stephen King

I struggled with depression from the pressures I place upon myself during the period of January 2020. Debts finally written-off. The freedom to push on came with a lull of what to do with my life. Up until this moment, I was confident and sure of the future. As it turned out to that was rather misplaced. I was still at a crossroad in my life. Decisions to make and a career to pursue.

Relationships had also been plaguing my mind. The psychic reading a few years ago often weighs on me. Knowing specific things but missing crucial information about where and how I will meet this person is a constant disruption to my thought process. I am perfectly fine on my own, but who would not want true unbridled happiness? If it is destined for me, then I sure as hell want to be a part of that life. Each day seems further from that reality.

For sceptics and non-believers of the supernatural, I urge you to skip this chapter. I would not want to offend your beliefs or push mine onto you. You are entitled to your views as I am mine. I respect each person's position on the subject.

I wrote a tongue-in-cheek post for my social media profiles:

So. I recently learnt that I am going to be happily married to a Julie/Jenny, she is around 5"6, dark hair - long slightly curly, and we will have a baby boy.

He wanders the streets aimlessly in pursuit of this Julie. Where she may be is anyone's guess and this poor soul is pathetically calling out loud enough for all to hear, "JULIE!"

People turn from all directions, looking at this man cradling a note as if his life depended on it. Little did they know, it did. This was his only glimmer of hope in a life of despair. Maybe there is no Julie after all, but for his sanity, it's best to believe and live in hope.

Where for art thou Julie

Some days I urge the forces that be to make this transition swift and let me have the future set out for me now. Other times I am content with life as it is at the moment. I enjoy my independence and freedom, and not being burdened by worrying about other peoples desires. I figure destiny and fate happen when they are supposed to. Right now, I may not be ready for such a transformation to mine and Jessie's lives.

I had been talking to a *Medium* without knowing her gift of communicating with those that had passed away. She had become a big supporter of my book *A Father's Daughter* and also the early draft of this book. She had made a connection with those around me which provided an opportunity for my step-dad to communicate along with premonitions. The connections were strong. My step-dad wanted to clarify a previously confusing message he had said via a different psychic. The topic of importance was marriage. I had thought that he had been light-heartedly mocking me, as I was so far from a fairytale ending it would be obscene, but he was telling me that it will happen. Not only that, but it will be a happy marriage. The fairytale will include a baby boy. A brother for Jessie. The one thing that she has wanted since forever. Of course, she would prefer that it happened between her mother and me, but it never did and certainly would not happen between us now.

Having something to look forward to on top of Jessie eventually returning home gives me solace and comfort among the many dark and low moments. It is easy to be despondent and self-critical at times, but I never allow myself to stay low for long. There is no benefit to it, just a repetitive cycle of no productivity in life. Instead, I delve into my interests, whether it be writing, web-design, or various entertainment sources. Occupying the mind is a great tool to change one's perspective.

She provided a damning assessment of Casey.

I agree, she wants you to suffer
Sick woman

The Medium then went on to flatter me.

I was just going to say that about you finding a woman. you forgot, likeable, knowledgeable and appealing in your description of you. Your step dad meant that he sees you as having a happy marriage in the future. I do spirit writing, talking to dead people. I also see people just after they die. I don't know why they come to me.

It was reassuring to hear a positive for my life.

That would be nice. I was so confused when he came through with that in my mums reading. I couldn't have been in a worse place in my life at that moment. So far from anything like that.

She revealed that he was present and communicating.

ummmm, I don't know how to say this but when I read that, he whispered in my ear what it meant. Spirits drive me crazy sometimes.

Talk then turned to my potential love interest. I had been told by the other psychic that I would be with a Jenny, which I also took as meaning Jennifer, however, this was potentially wrong.

Jennifer is not the girls name. She is about 5'6", dark hair, long a little curly. Starts with J but not Jennifer - Julie. You will have another child. A boy.

I was not very enthusiastic about having a boy. Not that I would love them any less if it does come true but they can be exhausting.

Oh god help us. boys are a handful.

She then had a message to pass onto me regarding my mum, me and Jessie.

Your mum: She was the best wife a man could have.

144

You: You were the best and he is proud of you. He doesn't want you to feel sad you weren't there at the end, remember him when he was well.

Jessie: He's sorry she saw him sick and wants her to know she was his princess.

The message meant the world to me. Whenever I hear of the love someone has for Jessie I become emotional. I want her to have all of the love in the world around her. When she loses someone that loves her dearly it is an incredible loss that I feel.

Thank you. Means a lot. Has me in tears. But means everything.

She did not want me upset and felt guilty for sharing.

Don't cry, I didn't want to upset you. When I talk to people they sometimes just come to me to give a message.

The medium then made a statement which typified my step-dad perfectly. He is where I get all of my strength and importance of family.

You know what is weird is not only did I hear him, but I felt him, like the love for you guys. It makes me get tingles up my back , my scalp gets a weird feeling, I feel nauseated and my heart feels like it is about to burst with love.

I shared my thoughts on his greatness.

He was an incredible family man. It's where I get my inspiration from. He would do anything for us at the drop of a hat.

She acknowledged how lucky we were to have had him in our life.

You were blessed to have him.

There are ways in which those that have passed try to communicate she explained.

145

Do you ever suddenly feel the hairs on the back of your neck stand up and a chill runs through you? He is definitely present.

A moment in my story made her uneasy. She had been reading the section where I attended a psyhcic reading with my mum. The part where I was pointed to as my step-dad relayed the message about me getting married. She had felt that too.

I am a little creeped out. What creeped me out was you were the one pointed as the person he was referring to. When talking about the message to you, I felt him pointing at you on the computer. This page kept repeating itself for the past few minutes. I'm freaked out.

I tried to encourage her to look after herself.

You may be better of skipping the chapter for now.

There was no stopping her.

no way.

Talk then switched to Casey. I had been informed previously that Connor and Casey would be having a child together one day even though she does not want any. I was now told that it would not happen.

Casey is not having a child with Connor

This was a shocking revelation. I had been under the impression that they would have a child.

The plot thickens. I would find it immoral if she did.

There was some uncomfortable news about Casey which I will not share. Needless to say it had me in tears.

26

SADNESS

Jessie had recently received an iPhone X for an early birthday present. Please don't ask me why a nine-year-old, going on ten, would need such an expensive device. It's illogical, but it appears as though her mother or Connor is trying to buy Jessie's love. My nephew David-James recently quipped similarly to me during a conversation at my mothers home. Most people can't afford to buy the phone outright in a single purchase which is nigh on one-thousand pounds. It would be fair to assume that it is a mobile phone contract. Based on the iPhone model and data, I would guess that it costs around £40-£50 each month. It's baffling that Casey can afford such an expensive luxury but not feel able to contribute to my considerable travel costs. A mobile phone on a cheaper monthly tariff would have been acceptable for Jessie. I don't begrudge her the gift but do think that Casey doesn't have her priorities in the right place. She put this distance between us, yet expects me to travel as though it doesn't cost anything while in reality, it's unaffordable for most people, myself included. Without my mums' support, it wouldn't be possible, and here Casey is gifting phones so casually.

"They are obviously trying to buy her love. She adores you, so that won't work." David-James remarked.

"It doesn't bother me either way. The winner in this is Jessie, and that makes me happy." I responded.

The reality is that Jessie gets flourished with gifts on occasion by her mother. It is rare, but when it happens, it does with a bang. "Beat that, Steve!" I am sure is the thought process. I do not play games of competition or have interest in one-upping anyone. I briefly explained to Jessie my thoughts on her owning an expensive phone.

"If mummy does get you an iPhone X that is a wonderful gift, and very expensive. So that you know, if I could afford one for you, I wouldn't get it. It's too much at your age. A great present, though."

I did not want her to feel bad about receiving the latest iPhone. Anyone would love to receive a phone of immense quality adults included. It trumps my phone. In comparison, mine is ancient, not by choice. Poor credit and bad decisions in the past have hindered me from getting a contract phone.

During the week, I received a text message from Jessie. She had supposedly acquired the new phone early. I had to verify whether it originated from her. She confirmed that it was which allayed any concern that someone had attempted to disguise themselves as her. It was a shock to hear that she had received the phone in January. Her birthday is not for a few more months. Why rush to give her the gift early?

I could not understand, nor would I spend any amount of time wondering. If it is a demonstration of love, then it is terrific. I can not help but feel that it is as a way to tie her to the place she is supposed to call home. In a couple of years, we all know where we are heading; directly into a new court hearing to overturn the previous decision. Get Jessie home with me where her heart continues to desire. I suspect she will hear the words, "You'll have to leave that here."

Like me, Jessie won't allow materialistic possessions to control her. When that time comes, she will be more mature and ready for expensive devices. At which point, I will provide her with what is needed and on occasion desired. I will not, however, buy her love, nor will I dictate how and where she can take her items. Hypothetical, of course. There may be no underlying message. Merely a genuine offering. Again, beautiful gift.

When I show compassion and care for Casey, it doesn't last long before I feel contempt. The reason for that is Jessie. Time and time again, she suffers, and there is nothing I can do about it, which hurts us both. Promises get her hopes up, only to be dashed and taken away. Casey had told Jessie that they would be coming down my way this upcoming weekend. It did not happen. Our Friday phone call was sombre with Jessie sad missing home. The tone of her voice was despondent. A couple of moments, I managed to raise a laugh from her, but it never stayed. Her mind would not focus away from the miserable time she was enduring.

Our phone call came from her new phone. Jessie tried to call with video chat. For the time being, I have made it clear that I only want a traditional phone call. Too many prying eyes and ears interfering.

"Hi Daddy," Jessie said with a sad and deflated look on her face.

"You know I don't like video calls. Can you call back normally."

"Damn it. Okay." Jessie replied.

The video chat cancelled, and the phone rang immediately. We continued talking as the call reconnected.

"Hello, girly."

"Hi."

"Are you sad that I wouldn't do a video chat?"

"Not really."

"Are you sure. You sounded sad?"

"Nah. I don't mind."

"What's up? You looked sad in the video chat, and don't sound too happy."

"Nothing," Jessie replied.

"Hmmm. Sounds like somethings bothering you," I said. Eager to understand what is going on with her, "So what have you been up to?"

"Not much."

"Surely you've done something. Nothing comes to mind?"

"Nope."

"I haven't done much myself. I started writing again. Tell you something funny. In that game, I play with the guns. Mason shot me by accident. So I chased after him and blew him up with a grenade. His was a genuine mistake, but I had to get revenge," I said while laughing, struggling to contain my joy as I recollected the moment as though it just happened.

Jessie laughed but offered nothing in the way of conversation.

"I spoke to Kerrie. She said you and Oakley are going to see each other when your back down here."

"Yay," Jessie said with a wave of excitement that had been missing from the start.

"I said, not this time we're busy."

"What?"

"Only joking, of course, you're going to see him. Was winding you up."

"Oh. Good then." Jessie said with relief.

"So what have you been doing?" I asked.

"Nothing," Jessie responded.

"Anything planned this weekend?"

"Nope."

"You have nothing to do at all this weekend?"

"No."

"So. This is mummy's weekend, but she doesn't bother to do anything with you?"

"Nope."

I took a moment to pause; wanting to avoid any further negatives. I was not impressed.

Flourishes her with an expensive gift, but makes no effort to interact. Her life is lonely without my family. I do not like witnessing such sadness.

151

"I can't think of much to raise your spirits. We'll see each other next weekend, so we have that to look forward too. Do you not have anything from Christmas you could play with?" I asked.

"No. Nothing."

"I would say do some writing, but that's my thing. Maybe try and find something different to do for a little while. Maybe do some drawing."

"Already done that."

It is staggering how different her world is from one household to the other. At my home, I am available to her whenever she wants to play or talk. The family resides nearby and convenient to visit at short notice. Everyone adores Jessie. By contrast, her life up north is only uplifted by school and friends. At home, she gets no attention from her mother. Sister Emma only plays on her terms which is rare in itself and hardly ever fun. They take Jessie for granted, and the only family nearby is Connors.

Emma is jealous of Jessie. I hear a lot as the weeks' progress, and it does affect me. She deserves so much better. One would expect the children to come together through the trauma they have endured of having their lives upheaved. Instead, Emma appears to have a vendetta and hell-bent on ruining Jessie's future. At least at this moment in time. Knowing her personality, I suspect this will last a lifetime. She is a mirror image of Casey, which is not comforting.

"Emma said something horrible to me."

"What has she said now," I asked

"She said, 'When your older and one day get married I'm going to tell your husband everything you have ever done wrong'," Jessie explained.

"That's not nice, but I'm hardly surprised. What did you say in response?"

"I said, 'Well if you get married I won't do anything like that to you'," Jessie said confidently

"That's good, don't go down to their level. I would've said something worse, but you're better than me."

"Yep." Jessie offered.

Our call came to an end a short while later. Jessie gets bored on the phone when the calls are too long, so we keep them short. It's the opposite to a year or so ago during court proceedings when I couldn't get her off of the phone. Now that we see each other often the phone calls are less significant. It is reassuring to hear each others voices in the interim. As soon as the phone call ended a message arrived on my phone from Jessie.

Miss you

27

COMMUNICATION

Telephone calls have been a cause for concern for some while. There has never been a settled routine even during Court. To this day, the times change without warning. I never know when to expect the phone to ring. As it is Jessie and I only talk on the phone twice a month. We used to have the calls on a Tuesday, which is every week so four times a month. It was proving impossible to get a settled routine. There was always something she was in the middle of whether it be a bath or Casey on that rare occasion would have ice-cream at the ready. Rather convenient and not a distraction tactic, I say with all the sarcasm in the world. Jessie has told me that this only happens when we have telephone calls.

Eventually, we switched the calls to Fridays, which would allow us to have a settled arrangement. It hasn't been any better, and the calls could connect anytime between 6 pm and 9 pm. How I am supposed to prepare dinner is beyond me. That's Casey for you, chaotic without structure. I've tried to switch it back, but she fights me at every turn. I don't see the point in having fewer phone calls a month if the quality of those calls is no different from before.

As I collect Jessie fortnightly from school on a Friday, we, of course, don't have a phone call on those days as we are already together. There will be a need in the foreseeable future to discuss telephone calls. Instability creates negativity which only degrades with time.

Jessie and I do have regular contact via Whats App, but it's not the same as speaking to one another. Hearing each other's voices, tones, and mannerisms aren't replicated by emojis and LOL's. It often dawns on me more frequently than I would care to admit that Casey could stop our messaging communications at any moment, and I wouldn't put it past her. For now, she obliges, which is a positive gesture and a step forward in putting Jessie first in her decision making, but for how long? Only she knows. For the most part, I think it is to win favour with Jessie by trying to sweeten her. Whatever the reason if it makes Jessie happier then I approve and of course it is benefiting me as I have a direct connection to Jessie. I have no interest in the I'm loved more than you nonsense. All of these expensive gifts recently from Casey don't phase me in the slightest. The winner in that is Jessie, and I am all for that.

One thing I do know is that you can't buy love. It doesn't work that way; all you can hope for is a short term gain. Acts of kindness and nurturing are the way to win someone's heart. A genuine sincerity. You either have it, or you don't. Insincerity unravels and reveals a deep resentment and mistrust. The person bearing gifts feels insulted that the recipient declines their gestures and ultimately flawed expectations. The recipient then sees what the gifts were for and feels used and nothing more than a store purchase. Only time will tell with that saga. I can see all hell breaking loose at some point though, and while I have no role in it, I am sure to be blamed somehow.

28

CONFUSION

Our lives are topsy turvy. Casey can be disruptive and manipulative and then demonstrates compassion and generosity. I received a text message from Casey offering an extended holiday with Jessie and asking whether she could travel down and bring her. My tough stance over Christmas had made an impact and gained the desired result. I never did mind Casey bringing Jessie. In-fact I could do with all the help I can get. The issue was Casey dictating to me and providing minimal notice. Now she is behaving fairly and maturely, and that is refreshing. There may be underlying reasons which are not for our benefit; Emma's desire to be in Chelmsford, maybe Casey has valentines day plans; either way, I am grateful.

I had wondered whether Casey was planning to travel in the holidays. Jessie had intimated that Connor bought tickets, however, Casey had made no suggestions to me before receiving the message. The recent excursions had taken a toll on my body. I felt relief that there would be a break on the horizon.

The suspect part of the message received was *Hi Stephen*. It is very formal and sent as though either her mother prepared the text or she has done it in such a way as to one day attach as evidence to show her as being reasonable.

There is a possibility that I am overthinking and should take it at face value. With Casey, though I have learnt that I always need to be on my guard and expect the unexpected. Too many times, innocuous things have come back to slap me in the face. Spending added time with Jessie is a blessing, which I am sure she will be thrilled about too. If there is more to it, then that can wait. Right now the focus is only on seeing Jessie and enjoying our time together.

I did not want to get caught out this time with travel plans, unlike last time when I had assumed Casey would also be collecting Jessie. I raised the question at the earliest opportunity for clarity to avoid any surprises while confirming my acceptance to her travelling.

That's generous. Thank you. Would you be collecting her for the return or do I need to make plans to get her back?

Thankfully, the response from Casey was swift. No playing games or messing around leaving the other side waiting. We were communicating efficiently.

No it's fine I'll be travelling back to collect Jessie and take her home.

Thoughts then turned to the upcoming weekend with Jessie. I do not like or feel comfortable without her home. I get on with my life, make strides with projects and hobbies but part of me is missing. The trouble is my body is exhausted, and the mind needs a rest. With Casey giving us the full week-long holiday together just a week after, maybe we could reluctantly miss the weekend contact. It would only be a week longer without seeing each other and save a lot of travel, money and provide time to regenerate. I wondered about Jessie's weekend and shared a short message exchange.

What have you been up to?

We went to a shopping centre

Get anything nice?

Yeah

I wanted to know Jessie's thoughts on the situation. Striking the right balance to get an honest answer is always tricky. Word it favourably to not travelling, and she may well agree and hide any sadness. On the flip side, choose the wrong phrasing, and she may feel compelled to say she misses me. I only wanted to hear what she wants without her feeling obligated to appease anyone. It should not matter what I or her mother desires. Yes, we have received an extended holiday, and maybe her mother deserves to have our weekend as a thank you. I have done this in the past. When the weekend arrives, I end up missing Jessie dearly but keep it to myself. I would not want her to feel bad for me or have that weight on her shoulders.

In the past, I have informed Casey before a holiday if there is an issue with travel. She always responds that Jessie will be fine. Yet, when I next see Jessie, it transpires that she was not okay at all. She had been sad about missing home, wishing that I had come for her. This time I decided to find out how Jessie is feeling directly before making a decision.

We have all the half-term together from the weekend after next. How would you feel if we didn't have next weekend?

I could sense an uneasy pause in Jessie's response. We had exchanged a few love emojis before me sending the message. I sent a quick follow up message encouraging Jessie to answer freely without guilt.

Just be honest. I want to know how you would feel.

Sad

Okay. I'll come

Yay

Before I had asked her whether she would be okay, I had no idea. Sometimes she will be comfortable for a short period if there are plans in place to keep her busy. It is the mundane and uneventful lifestyle that makes our separation worse for her. It felt great to make her happy. To know that when she said *sad*, she meant it. She would have been feeling such a lull at that moment. Maybe her day had been pleasant, and I lowered her mood enough to make her heart drop. Remedying it promptly, by bringing her joy and relief made me happy. Sadly to get an honest reaction, there will be lows along with the highs. Of course, she would not want to be sad; however, if that is how she feels, then it is what we must endure.

We then shared a thoughtful exchange. When such a vast distance separates us, it is the best we can hope.

Love You

Love You

It is rather sad that Jessie would feel so much pain at not coming home for the weekend. She is more than aware of how arduous the journey was for both of us when she made that statement. It is long and an incredible grind. We would be seeing each other the following week anyway, but yet in her own words, she would be *sad*. That says it all to me after all of this time away. She is living a new life for the past couple of years now — almost three years. Jessie is unsettled. To this day, she still grasps and clings to any opportunity to come home. I owe it to her to strive to make that happen whenever possible. If some moments are harder than others, then that is part of our story to endure.

I wanted to make Jessie smile, and I knew just the trick and set up to achieve that goal. Often when she says, "How dare you?" I would respond, "Oh, I do dare." which results in her calling me *cheeky*. Secretly she loves it. I knew when I said "How dare you?" what her response would be. She would grab the opportunity to use the "Oh I do dare." on me finally, and boy would it bring a smile drawn across her face. The conversation started with me enquiring whether she has done any reading lately.

Done any reading lately?

Nope (laughing emoji)

How dare you

Oh I do dare (thumbs up and laughing emoji)

We both shared a laughing emoji. It was an inside joke that only we would understand, and now you do too. I had hoped that Jessie would have been reading. I had bought the entire Harry Potter collection of books and many others. I made a light hearted joke in response to her lack of reading.

I'm going to lock you in a library.

The situation with having Jessie home for the weekend worsened. Finances were tighter than ever. Affording the

162

costs for travel had a devastating impact on grocery shopping. I had already told her that I will be coming. I never want her to live with doubt or having to second guess anything that I say. Meals are becoming scarce due to a food shortage at home which is not a comfortable situation for anyone to endure. I suffer for Jessie in more ways than anyone could understand.

29

THREATENED

February 2019 started with a bang. A typical weekend contact concluded in spectacular drama after a long drive too. No thought or care for the hardship endured or the sacrifice required. I had attempted to avoid this weekend contact. The travel had become arduous, and a break would do my body wonders, especially as Jessie was coming down the following weekend to stay for an entire week. In contrast to just a Saturday, we usually get after taking away the travel time. She did not want to miss our weekend.

Jessie ran out of school, screaming with excitement as she slammed into me with a hug and a kiss. An embrace that most would wish for, I was the epicentre of her world.

I made a whimsical remark as we walked to the car, "You made me travel all the way up here."

"Yeah, I missed you." She responded.

I had been correct in my assessment that she had needed me. My mum felt that she might be okay for a week, but I knew Jessie better than anyone. She lets me into her innermost thoughts, fears and hearts desires. All of my senses had told me to get her home. She needed me, and here I am coming to her rescue. The glow on her face stayed for moments longer than usual. She was proud of me for coming, and I delighted to be here for her. As exhausting as it is, there has never been a moment where I have regretted a journey.

The weekend itself was of no more significance than any other, although Jessie wanted to soak up the time together by offering plenty of hugs and kisses. It was a typical reunion. We enjoyed watching a few teen comedy movies which she loved. Not quite a teenager yet, in-fact she has a few more years, but she can relate with school and her friends.

Unbeknown to me, Casey had sent photos to my home through Jessie. They consisted of pictures of Jessie and Emma. Considering before Court proceedings and during there were accusations that I had emotionally abused Emma, it would seem strange that now I was receiving photos of her. I wondered what game Casey is playing? I pondered this question to a few people, none of them could provide a conclusive answer; she's trying to make you miss Emma, to annoy you and get a reaction, or to try and make Jessie miss their home.

I had no issues with Jessie having photos. It just seemed suspicious after all this time. Why now?

"I don't know why mummy has sent those photos to my home," I said.

Jessie was equally confused, "I don't know, but I got them to print a photo of us."

165

"Why would they print a photo of me?" I asked.

"Because I wanted it," Jessie said enthusiastically.

"It is a nice photo, but I don't understand the photo of Emma. Of course, if you want the photo, I have no problem with you having it."

Jessie looked at the photo, not entirely understanding why she had it with her — bundled in amongst the pictures of us and a beautiful school portrait of just her.

"We both know mummy is going to ask you what I thought of the photos when you get back."

"Yeah probably straight away."

"Not sure that quick, but she will. Just say that I didn't understand why she sent the photo, but it's fine for me to have it."

"No. I can't say that."

"Why can't you say that. It's the truth."

"I can't; she will moan. I don't like saying bad things about you."

"It's not a bad thing. If you keep saying I like everything mummy will think it's fine."

"She will moan at me, and won't stop."

"This is frustrating," I ordered. I then took a moment to think, "Do you want your phone charged?"

"No. It's fine."

"How comes? Is it because of everyone bothering you?"

"Yep."

"Do you not want to talk to them?"

"Nope," She replied with confidence and ignorance of the parties concerned. Evident that Jessie puts up with them

166

because she has to, but away and free, she has no desire to communicate on any level. Not even a simple emoji or wave hello.

"Okay, well, it's up to you. You can always charge it."

That was the end of that conversation. If Jessie wanted to tell me more about her reasons or what was bothering her, she would. I had no intention to probe her for information. Witnessing her content, relaxing and enjoying time in her bedroom made me happy.

The day went by in a breeze. I introduced her to *The Breakfast Club* movie. A classic teen movie from the '80s. We had watched *Easy A* yet again. Jessie had taken a liking to Emma Stone's movies almost as much as I had taken a liking to Emma Stone. Within the film was a reference to some of the cult classic teen comedies from yesteryear, one of which was the fantastic *The Breakfast Club*. She enjoyed the film, though some parts I skipped for obvious reasons, namely the sexual innuendo moments. They were not appropriate for her to hear at her age.

It was not the day we had planned or expected, but we made the most of it even with the limited time together. The plan in place was that Jessie would visit Oakley at his home on Saturday. It was not my idea, but my sister Kerrie's. When we arrived home on Friday after an extensive journey, my mum informed us that we are still on for tomorrow. I had not heard, nor had I attempted to communicate between then and now as I had been busy and distracted. To know that it was still happening was a relief. More so since I had informed Jessie a week prior, which had her excited.

I text my sister on the morning of Saturday to enquire whether it is still okay for us to come round. I was surprised to receive a response explaining that they are out for the day but will return home at 4 pm. At which time she will get in touch. Shortly after that time, I was shocked to hear that she was now too tired to entertain Jessie. To put it bluntly, I was fuming. It would be the last time I allow anyone to get Jessie's hopes up and then dash them so harshly. She is not a yo-yo or someone else's play toy. I phoned mum and explained my disdain at the situation. Surely a single hour would have been okay, but to have nothing and been left on tenterhooks all day was disgusting. Mum agreed, but we kept it to ourselves. No longer will I make plans for Jessie in advance with anyone. They can wait until nearer the time when we know our plans in future. It will be on our terms, not anyone else's.

We put the disappointment behind us although Jessie did take a short while to get over it. She had been looking forward to spending time with her cousin, and I am sure he was looking forward to their moment together too. We made the most of the day spending our time at home. Cuddles and laughs were shared. Other people may let Jessie down, but she knows that I will always be there for her.

Sunday morning was frustrating for Jessie. We had had a late night on Saturday. An attempt to make the day last forever, but eventually we both fade off into the realm of sleep deprivation. To my horror, she was awake long before me. When I briefly opened my eyes, she was sitting up anxious for me to rise from bed. It was not the day for that. I needed my rest, and I knew it too. I needed to make sure I can make these trips. She watched TV and played in her bedroom while I gained a few more winks.

When I arose, Jessie was engrossed in her TV shows. By this point, my sleeping or waking made no difference to her. We had breakfast, the sports panellists talking on TV did not interest her. I only kept it on as I knew that she would be back in her bedroom shortly after eating.

"Is this boring you?"

"Yeah. I'm looking at the bookshelf as the books are more interesting."

I gave out a laugh. To think that Jessie would instead look at a bookshelf while eating her breakfast than the TV was funny. On the other hand, she was not impressed when I increased the volume of the TV to hear the panellists. Her boredom had changed to irritation. She gave me a look of 'Are you for real?' I smiled.

We did not have long together before it was time to leave. Our routine is to head off around lunchtime. It is a long journey and time is needed to fit in a food break along the way. My nephew David-James often travels with us on Sunday journeys. This time was no different; we collected him from his home and made a final visit at mums home to say farewell. It is nice for her and Jessie to see each before we depart. One last hurrah, or stealing of the snacks whatever way you want to look at it. We do raid the cupboards without remorse. Mum is like a deer trapped in the headlights, too slow to keep up.

Filling the car with fuel was an unenviable task as Jessie wanted snacks. The filling station had limited stock. To her surprise, I turned off a little way up the road to visit another shop to gather some goods for the trip. She was thrilled to have sweets and drinks for the journey. We all grabbed what we wanted, paid and got back on the road. Ten minutes lost, but food gained and worth the deviation. It would have been an arduous trip without anything to drink or eat before we stop at the motorway services, which was two hours away. I try to split the journey in half as best as possible. It is not a perfect science, but I know the route, and we have regular services we use. I know the expensive ones to avoid and the ones we like to visit. It is our routine.

Snacks were shared and devoured throughout the car journey north. Jessie had not charged anything before the ride which did not impress me. I had tried to charge the Nintendo Switch, but I had only put it in the dock a few minutes before we left home. She had played it throughout the previous evening and left it lying around. Now she was stuck in the car with no charger and a depleting battery. Jessie miraculously managed to get half of a journey out of it. Since getting a Nintendo Switch, it has been her go-to device for the trip. She enjoys Crayola Scoot. The player skates around a skate park plastering everywhere with fluorescent paint. Skills and boosts enhance the gameplay, and players can customise characters with clothes. Jessie loves the game and rarely plays the more expensive titles in her collection.

I repeatedly asked Jessie to get her phone out and charge it. She had not wanted to use it all weekend, but I needed it to be ready for when it is time to update her mother on our time of arrival. It is impossible to use mine while driving not only because it is against the law, but I use the map feature as a sat-nav. Although I know the journey, I find I can focus more with it on, and it breaks the journey down into three sections; around eighty miles between them. I use these benchmarks to make the trip tolerable. For instance, when we come off of the M25 onto the M1, it is close to eighty miles on the one stretch of road. A monotonous drive of the same constant meandering motorway. It is easy to lose one's sanity on such mundane travel. We stop at the services at roughly half of this stretch. There are three within proximity to one another, ten miles or so separating each which at full speed equates to a ten-minute gap. The decision is made based on factors such as daylight, tiredness, hunger and the need for a toilet break. I often prefer to push on to get the most out of the day.

We stopped at Northampton services for a much-needed rest and filled our stomachs even though we had consumed plenty of crisps and sweets along the way. Big-Mac's awaited David-James and me, while Jessie chose her predictable option of a Chicken Nugget Happy Meal. She used this moment to provide a few cuddles and be close to me. Being stuck in a car like sardines is hardly the same. Jessie places so many things by her feet in the car that she is overwhelmed. Why she does not put some on the backseat, I will never know. We took a quick toilet break and recommenced our journey.

As we set off, I again informed Jessie to charge her phone. I only remember at random moments. More often than not, my mind is solely focused on the road ahead and the constant flurry of cars behind. Fast travel with no room for error. It is exhausting on every part of my body. Legs are aching, and hands crunched around the steering wheel for hours on end. Then the eyes bare the brunt of straining excessively, which often brings on mild headaches. It can be overwhelming for prolonged periods, but I have become accustomed to it.

I was shocked to find that Jessie had not charged her phone as we approached within twenty miles of our destination. After numerous requests, I was agitated. She could sense my angst and hastily connected the phone to the charger. She always felt that there was plenty of time to do it, but she was wrong. It was taking longer and longer to charge when finally the screen glowed in the dark. We were not far, though, and time was running out to relay our ten-minute lateness before her mother leaves her house. Eventually, Jessie said "Sent." I was relieved. Not the best timing but at least she had sent the message.

Around five minutes out from the destination, Jessie's phone rang from an unknown number. Based on the timing, it was more than likely related to this situation. I informed Jessie to answer the call. She fumbled. By the time she went to retry swiping, the call had ended. Not, the end of the world, we had almost arrived. Only a few short roads remained.

As we approached the drop off location in the car, there was no-one visibly around. Although we were slightly late, it appeared as though we were early compared to the receiving party. Connor soon emerged from the darkness of the park. Behind in tow was Casey. Connor did not take a moment's hesitation in moving within proximity of the vehicle. I had opened Jessie's car door as she was rummaging around her belongings, trying to organise what she needs to take with her. Three times Connor tried to interfere "You all right, Jessie." Not once did he receive a response. I am sure it damaged his pride. He took a moment and then turned his attention to me.

"Next time mate, can you let us know if you're running late?"

"Jessie sent a text," I replied

Casey interjected, "I didn't receive anything."

"Well, she sent it. You can check the phone if you want," I responded sarcastically.

"You don't have to get defensive Steve!" Connor said with an egotistical smile.

He knew it would irritate me, and it did. Finally, the manipulator showed his face. For too long, I have seen through him, but he tries to play the good-boy routine. "Have a safe trip back." My ass. It would seem it is okay for them to speak out, but as soon as I responded in defence of myself, it is wrong. A brief stare at one another ensued. I had been ready for his attitude for a long time, and I guess he had been waiting for his moment too. Maybe me responding to Casey in a tone he did not like bothered him. Only he knows, but after they walked off to head on home, he returned to my car. By this time, I settled in the driver's seat almost ready to recommence the journey South.

I wound the window down. Connor wanted to have a conversation, but he seemed more interested in attempting to dictate to me and provide words of wisdom. I had no interest in what he had to say. My opinion is that Connor should have no involvement during Jessie's transition between parents. He makes situations tenser. Speaking about Jessie piqued my interest and garnered a reaction back.

"Jessie is nine years old; it isn't good to argue in front of her." He explained. The contradiction is that he was blaming me for an argument he had started. He may be used to twisting words with others and playing mind games, but I am too intelligent for him. It will not work with me.

"Don't tell me about my daughter. I know her better than anyone." I ordered.

"Well she is nine, and has a mum, okay," Connor responded.

I looked briefly at him and shrugged my shoulders. I am sure in hindsight; my facial expression said whatever because I could not understand what he was trying to say. Relaying to me my daughter's age and the fact she has a mother is moronic. Of course, I am aware of it; I had just seen her mum just a moment ago, and I was in the delivery room supporting Casey when Jessie was born. I'm aware of her age.

He was not happy that he could not intimidate or manipulate me and left a parting shot.

"Just behave." Connor threatened.

"Behave?" I asked curiously.

"Behave or else," He said while walking away, in an attempt to leave with the last word.

I shouted from the car, "OR ELSE WHAT?"

That was the end of our interaction. I had not only seen Connor for the manipulative character that he is but also the bully. For too long he had been encroaching on the handovers making himself the main party present — overbearing and manipulative, hardly positive traits. When Casey and I are together without other parties involved, it is amicable and effortless. When others attend, she steps back and lets them reign free. Trying to tell me about Jessie was a non-starter immediately. That was the worst move he could do, or maybe it got the reaction he expected. It's strange to think that Jessie had been saying a while ago that Connor wants to shake my hand and now this happens. All that time, I knew it was a move to try and be controlling. Be all nice, while manoeuvring everything to his benefit. He does not intimate me, nor do I care what he thinks, but he has just provided an opportunity to exploit. They play mind games with me all of the time. Threatening me with "Or Else," was his mistake. He went a step too far because he could not control himself. He was losing the situation so lashed out.

On the way home, I pulled into a filling station to provide an opportunity to send Casey a message before I get stuck driving. I needed to get this out of my head and onto the phone.

So. Your boyfriend just threatened me. For some time now he has interfered with handovers which is none of his business. He even tried to educate me on Jessie and manipulate my responses. Not going to happen. I will be liaising with my solicitors this week. At no point have you ever been threatened. I won't be putting up with it. A handover should be a safe environment for all parties. There is no place for unhinged people. He said or else, I replied or else what? I've known he is a bully for sometime and now he has shown his real colours. I worry for our daughters welfare in his presence.

I wanted my disdain at his behaviour to be on record and with Casey at the earliest opportunity. She responded in her typical fashion of twisting the situation around trying to make me out to be the one causing problems. She even went as far as insinuating that Connor never said anything. That was another mistake. They had not realised that my nephew David-James had been present. He is small and was gathering his belongings at the time but saw and heard everything. I sent a follow-up text message in response to Casey when I arrived at mums home as I usually do on the way back.

David was a witness and saw and heard everything. Jessie is terrified of him but tells me not to say anything but don't worry, it's all written down. You know she wants to live with me but she don't tell him because she is scared for him to know. He should not be at handovers it's not his position to be involved or to the extent that he is. You allow

him to dictate and don't embrace Jessie yourself. I will be talking to my
solicitors in the morning.

Again Casey responded by making out Connor to be a
Saint. Her words were falling on deaf ears as I already knew
too much about him to sway any opinions. In an attempt to
defuse the situation early, I sent Casey a reasonable
arrangements offer which she decided not to respond too.
More than likely because I suggested it and not her. She has
to be in control.

The arguing needs to stop. Will you agree in future handovers are just
between you, Jessie and I? People can support from a distance but it
shouldn't be so complicated. Jessie's phone may not have had internet
as I was asking her all the time to charge it but she left it so late. She
may not have connected to my phone which explains why you may not
have received the message. We could argue forever and pick at each
other or just do things civil. We don't need to like each other to just
pass her between each other for the best part of 10 seconds.

When no response was received I wanted to clarify a few
things so another message was sent.

I've spoken to a lot of people and they've said as step-parents they
don't get involved in handovers. It's about being respectful of boundaries
and allow Jessie to transition smoothly without drama. He has no legal
rights to Jessie whatsoever so his opinion is nothing on any level whether
he likes it or not. Courts wouldn't be interested in him and if you had
been honest throughout court I would've made sure he wasn't present
during handovers but you acted like he was nothing. I would encourage
him to have a child of his own if he wants a say on their life. For too
long he has overstepped boundaries getting too close and acting like he
is the most important person there even though he is the most irrelevant.

I never got involved with Emma and her dad. Wasn't my place to interfere.

Monday morning after waiting a few hours for Casey to respond to no avail, an email was sent to my solicitors. I attached copies of my messages and an explanation of what had happened and how I hope to proceed. Later in the day, I received a detailed email from them. They understand all that I endure along with the people and personalities involved.

Hi Steve,

I think it is right that handovers should now just be between you and Casey with Connor standing well back. Would be much better for Jessie too...

It was nice to hear a legal expert agreeing with my opinion of how to proceed with handovers and that I had not been overbearing or controlling. Of course, that is how they try to twist words and situations onto me. The perfect narcissists that they are. Now I had the law on my side, well at the very least the opinion of a law expert. If it does not make a difference at this moment, it will be useful for when we inevitably end up back in Court.

I captured a screenshot on my phone from the opening of the message from my solicitors. I then attached it to a message for Casey. I explained the advice I had received and that it would be in everyone's interest to move forward respectfully or I could get a letter sent if she prefers it to be official. A letter costs money and would be detrimental for her as it would be an official document which would then be on file if we were to return to Court. Casey never did respond. She often chooses ignorance when she feels backed into a corner and doesn't like the circumstances offered. Casey behaves similar to a child who covers their eyes when something scares them in the hope that it tricks the mind that it isn't happening. It's not real. She ignores and pretends it never happened. Except it has happened and she will be in for a shock if she suggests travelling in future.

I'm not afraid of Connor or any of Casey's family. I wanted her to feel what it's like when someone exaggerates and causes unnecessary havoc. It was just a mirror of what she has put me through for so long. A single moment for me to grab the opportunity with both and arms and say "You messed up." Let her see how it feels. I didn't drag it out for long, but it felt good to get one up over Connor. He didn't bother me, and he knew it too. His feeble threat was him flinching as he hadn't been able to control me.

Jessie later explained to me that Connor had told Casey that he never threatened me. Casey had been reacting to me on what he had been saying. She is a compulsive liar, so I never believe anything she says, but now he has revealed himself to be a liar too. The trouble with liars is that once a liar always a liar. The question is, what has he told Casey from the moment they met? And how manipulative has he been during that period until now? I suspect he has been deceitful. Maybe that explains the sleepovers Jessie has with Casey in the living room. An excuse to avoid friction in the bedroom. My interest only extends to Jessie and how it affects her. What they do within their relationship beyond her I honestly couldn't care less. They deserve each other.

30

ANIMOSITY

Relations soured by the day. While I try to restore some peace and order, there is a part of me fed up with continuing dialogue. I hate witnessing Jessie stuck in the middle of this mess between us, and I sincerely hoped that the parties involved keep her out of the drama. She does not need to know about the fire that burns between us. I have always cared about Casey, far beyond anything she deserves. That spark fades as I grow tired of her manipulation and accusations. For too long, there have been issues after issues — a cascade of drama that never needs to happen. When we are alone together, there is no such drama. A mutual understanding. Why then can we not just all get along and transition Jessie's life from one home to another in a calm and friendly manner? Connor and Casey's family obstruct and negatively influence her decisions. Without them, she is approachable and understanding. Regardless of whether their behaviour dictates the negativity, it is on her for allowing it to happen.

It is not something that I can remedy alone, and I am confident that the other parties will always place their agendas before Jessie. When our focus is on different things there can never be common ground. My eye is solely on Jessie. One-upping others takes second fiddle to her. Yes, I would love nothing more than to see Connor in jail. I despise him more and more every day. I can see through him and the strings he pulls in Casey's life. Would I go to any length to make that happen? Of course not. I do not care enough about him to give him much thought. It just pops into my mind from time to time - the ultimate revenge. We all have moments like that, whether we care to admit it. If he ever tries to reconcile and shake my hand, he will find his time wasted. I do not offer fake gestures or pretend niceties. For Jessie's sake, I would nod and smile.

A few days had passed since I tried to communicate with Casey via text message. She chose ignorance in a petty, childish fashion. Leave me waiting, and hope for a reaction. Sadly for her, I had said that all I had to say. All that I required from her was either an acceptance that Connor would not be interfering with handovers in future or decline and place him in a compromising situation. Either way, I guess for her there is no victory unless she can come up with a curveball. Maybe this is her reason for silence as Casey concocts something to change the tide into her favour. As it is if she agrees to my terms which work out for everyone, then she has conceded defeat. Continuing to allow Connor to appear at handovers to annoy me would not look favourable in Court, nor would it be a good situation for

Jessie to experience. Add this to the unpredictable nature of the man. Can he behave, or would he cause more chaos and potential headaches for Casey? It is all a quandary which she must weigh up and then decide upon a course of action. She may have been smug during our early message exchanges, but now reality would have kicked into the disruption Connor caused by being unhinged. If only he had kept quiet and not been confrontational. Somehow I think he was always going to fire off at some point. It just so happened to be recently.

As my birthday approached in just a couple of days I could not help but wonder whether Casey was waiting to ruin it with an argument. For this reason I decided that any communications for now would wait until Friday, the day after my birthday. Jessie was due to travel down on Saturday so there was no need for us to communicate before then anyway. So long as I am available to know where and when to collect Jessie then that would be all I need at this moment. Connor is not expected to travel as he never does, although with all that has been happening it would not surprise me if he decides to travel on this occasion to make a point. It would be pointless for the sake of ten seconds. The length of time it takes me to walk up to Casey, collect Jessie and walk back to the car. Moving forward transitions will be swift with no reason to engage with one another. My solicitor advised me not to react to anything as that is their angle. They need that from me. I will not oblige. Simplicity is bliss.

I had a few interesting engagements with people on Twitter, most of whom had experienced a similar situation to what I was enduring. The overriding consensus was that Jessie is being abused in her mothers care, whether directly or indirectly. The regular berating of me within proximity of her is not child-focused and abhorrent. Jessie feels the need to come to my aid confronting her mother and Connor even though I am not there to hear the slants against me. It does not go down well as they then levy their anger towards her until she cries. It is truly disgusting and even more disturbing is their lack of acknowledgement. They continue to portray the perfect home and family life.

Tactics were employed to get a reaction from me. With every passing day, week and month, the opportunity for me to get Jessie home comes nearer. They know that too and lose a little power a bit at a time. They need something to change the course of the inevitable outcome. Disrupting me is their only real hope. To that end and the fact that Casey was playing the childlike game of putting her hands over her ears to pretend she can't hear anything which in-turn fails to render a response, I sent a new text message which needed no reply.

As you have not responded or agreed for handovers to be safe for all parties I will no longer attend handovers in person. Jessie and I will say our goodbyes in the car and a witness will always travel with me and return her into your care. Every handover will be video recorded, with each recording deleted upon a successful handover.

The new routine covers all of the bases. I do not travel the length of the country and back again to encounter drama or to find Jessie stuck in the middle. Her transition between homes should be effortless, and this paves the way for that to happen. It is frustrating that it had to come to this, but tensions were escalating, and the mother was not coming up with a solution. Not long ago, I used to return Jessie from the car. My attempts to move on from that proved to be in vain as we were now back to square one. Going forward, this would be the permanent routine. They can not be trusted, and there is no way ahead trying to be amicable with people who only want to play games.

To my surprise I received a swift response from Casey. She was still pretending nothing happened even though she had not been present when he had returned to my car.

You weren't threatened, I'll be in contact when I know the times for Saturday.

I responded with a continuation of what happened and the expectations for the upcoming handover.

Behave yourself or else! Sounds like a threat to me. He waffled on that Jessie has a mother too which seemed absurd as I had literally just seen you. Of course she has a mum. Idk. I'll send someone to collect her when I have the details.

Amongst all of the agro and bickering, I do not understand Connors involvement during Jessie's transition into her mothers care. There is no reason why he and I should have any contact. I do not need to know him on a personal level. He is Casey's love interest, that is all. He seems to forget his place, acting more significant than his actual role. I have been there myself as a step-parent, doing the day to day activities. The significant differences here are that he played

184

an active role in not only Casey leaving me but also relocating our daughter across the country. I played no part in the ending of the relationship between Emma's father and Casey. I arrived in their lives to help pick up the pieces and be supportive at a chaotic moment in their lives.

Although I had a more significant impact on Emma's life than her father, I never forgot my place in the hierarchy. He was unreliable and lacked interest in his daughter, but she was his daughter. I was her mother's new partner. When it was time for him to collect Emma, I never got involved. Sometimes Casey wanted me to, but I refused. There had to be boundaries. It was not my place to interfere. This moral compass seems lost on Connor. He takes it upon himself to be the centre of attention. One would think he was the one being collected and returned. Neither Jessie nor I have any interest in him when he is there. When Jessie does leave my care, she chooses him over her mother, but I think that demonstrates the contempt she has for her mother rather than an adjuration for Connor.

We all have many years ahead of us living with the status quo, which sounds like hell to say out loud. To be this far on, almost three years from Jessie's abduction and have no common ground moving forward is surreal. If we can not get along by now then sadly we never will. It is a realisation that I am beginning to accept. It may not be ideal and indeed not a fantastic position for Jessie to find herself, however, by understanding the limitations and the disruptive personalities plans can be put in place to work around without constant disruption. Finding ourselves apart with minimal contact will go some way to limiting any negative encounters. There may be misunderstandings along the way, but I guess that comes with the territory. Can not have it all our way. There has to be a level of give-and-take.

This moment was a significant turning point in mine and Jessie's life. I had genuinely cared about her mother up to this point. Throughout our relationship, I had supported Casey through crucial moments in her life, but now I could finally see what everyone else had been seeing all of this time. A selfish and manipulative individual with no care for anyone but herself. I had always blamed everyone else around her, but now my eyes were open. There was no going back now. In a moment where her boyfriend overstepped a line by threatening me, rather than apologise to me and have a word with him, she made me out to be a liar. Her view was that he had not said anything which should not have come as a surprise as it was the same manipulative lying behaviour she had shown throughout Court. She was the victim, and I was to blame for everything. Rather than have him stand back during handovers which would make everyone feel comfortable, she would not agree to such a move. Instead, there was no choice but to keep my distance from handovers altogether. Whose best interests does that serve? Connors, of course. He does not have to feel left out, while Jessie has to hastily say her goodbyes from the car as I look on after as she walks to her mother. Wonderful..

31

HOLIDAY WEEK

Jessie and I got to spend an entire week together in early February 2020. She would be travelling south with her mother and Emma. It makes a change to have a break from travelling, but as always when Casey visits, she doesn't update me with a travel schedule. I went to bed on Friday night rather late. There was no indication of expected arrival time, which could have been any time during Saturday. Without an estimated time of departure, I assumed that it would likely be in the afternoon or evening. After all, who would expect someone to meet them with short notice in the morning? Before I went to bed, I sent Jessie a text message in the early hours of the morning just in case she ends up travelling while I'm asleep. I wouldn't want her to feel as though I am ignoring her if she doesn't get a reply.

Had a late night, 4am and I'm going to sleep. If you message me on the train and don't get a reply you'll know daddies asleep. I don't have a clue what time your coming so guess we'll see when I wake up. Have a fun journey, love you.

I awoke just after 9 am blurry-eyed, not awake but in a state of delirium. Instinctively I reached out for my phone which was within reach on the bedside cabinet. While checking the time, I noticed a Whats App notification. To my surprise, Jessie and Casey had both sent me messages. Both stated that they were due to arrive at 10 am, which was in less than an hour. Jessie had also attempted to call which failed. Not the best start to the holiday, and yet another demonstration of Casey's chaotic behaviour. Surely she would have known the previous day or even earlier in the week the time she would be arriving. Madness to throw a time at me at the last minute and expect me to be punctual. Her choice of location makes it all the more troubling. I have to endure a thirty-minute drive to the designated destination, which is ridiculous in itself. Nothing is preventing her from coming closer to my home.

My nephew David-James had agreed to travel and attend the handover with me earlier in the week, but for him to this was short notice. Phone calls to him went unanswered. He would later call me as soon as he woke, which by then was too late. It wasn't his fault, how could he know what time it would be when even I was caught off-guard. My brother David accompanied me instead. He wasn't best pleased, having just ordered a McDonalds breakfast delivery. I had no-one else available to attend with me. Casey had a history of playing up in our hometown for her families benefit. Throughout Court, she was a nightmare. I don't take any chances. If it weren't for David, I would have had to attend on my own and risk an incident without a witness. Her

188

family are unstable and never place Jessie first. Who knows how they would behave?

32

HEARTBREAK

Jessie opened up to me about how sad she feels. The night before returning her, she squeezed my hand and said, "I don't want to go home. I love you." She was sincere and heartbroken. The despondent look on her face and the furlong voice made me want to cry, but I held it in and remained stable. Instead, I hugged her, kissed her head and affectionately replied, "I love you too."

The day of her return, she cuddled up close to me on the sofa at my mums home. We had spent the night at her house, much to Jessie's delight. She was becoming anxious about the time running out before we have to leave. Her desperation is a concern. A child should not have to live with such torment and worry. To be anxious that our time is going too fast reveals the mental burden she endures. By all accounts, her home life is nothing short of challenging. Her sister Emma only cares about herself; Jessie is a burden in her life. Casey isn't comfortable around the children for long periods, so she regularly gets pushed aside and sent to her room, where again Emma makes it uncomfortable.

Connor can be charming and aloof, which Jessie enjoys. Sadly his mood can change in an instant. Play can swiftly end with "Go to your room now!" Such a sad state of affairs when there is no-one at home with a stable personality. The entire household filled with awkward and unstable people. Hardly surprising that she would cling to me for dear life. I give her stability and affection. She knows I will always be her stable anchor.

We did have a short conversation about how challenging it is living up North with dysfunctional people. I, of course, didn't use that word, but it does sum them up wonderfully. Casey doesn't like it when I say, "Treat it as a holiday." And I can understand why, but what else can I say to someone that does not want to be there. I am hardly going to say, "Bad luck; suck it up and deal with it." I will ease the burden from her and not make her feel trapped. A holiday is temporary. There is always an end and a return to home. She desires to come back to me, so a holiday makes sense in that regard.

If the home is unpredictable, then the best stability she can hope for now is from her friends. I emphasised to her that by focusing on friends, it would help her deal with the separation. I don't want her pining for me every moment of the day for weeks and months on end. It does her no good, and will cause her to deteriorate mentally. There must be some positives she can take from her life up North and friends are the best option. They are stable, loyal, and a constant in her life. Cling to them, have fun and take each day as it comes.

I then asked how she was getting on at school, and in particular in class. Jessie revealed to me something which I had not been aware of until this moment. I don't even think her mother or Connor knew about it. Her teacher, Mrs Candy often pulls her to one side and speaks in private at the back of the classroom about any issues concerning Jessie. I can't say what they talk about with specifics as I don't know myself. I didn't press Jessie for information. If she wished to share the information freely, then she would. I prefer to leave her to talk to me when she is ready. The conversation between Jessie and Mrs Candy is between them. To go out of her way to speak with Jessie, it would seem that Mrs Candy has noticed her sadness in class. One thing Jessie did tell me was that Mrs Candy had only been doing this since the parents evening I had attended. During the session, I had explained a little about the detachment Jessie feels and how she often struggles in silence. To hear that her teacher had taken it upon herself to get involved was comforting. I resent that Jessie doesn't have someone neutral in her life to open up about her troubles.

We had fun in-between the adoring moments.

Jessie likes to prove her strength and courage challenging me to a play fight. While I was on the floor, Jessie stood up in a fighting stance punching her fists forward and back in the air. I assured her that she would not want to challenge me, but she did want a challenge.

As I tried to stand, she pushed me back. When I pretended to lean in, she would lunge back in desperation. She was brave until I engaged. I made it clear that if I want to get her down on the floor, I could. She was on a high of bravado. Finding my smugness misplaced yet she was the one mistaken. I have a way of getting her to collapse in a heap with the slightest of touches. As she came close, I used just my fingers to press into the sides of her waist, which made her body spasm backwards. At that moment, I leapt up and pinned her down on the floor. She was in hysterics laughing, trying to fend me off as I pretended to throttle her. I call it throttling, but it is nothing more than me placing my hands loosely around her neck, and shaking gently. She finds it amusing. I had shown the guardian the technique during court proceedings previously to avoid any exaggerated accusations from the mother. The guardian then remarked, "That's not throttling" with a visible smile. She could see that Jessie and I play together. No-one gets hurt.

33

SADNESS

The emptiness of my home is apparent upon returning without Jessie. For just that single week it had felt like home. A place as if nothing had ever happened. We were back together, enjoying the little moments without feeling rushed or pressured to make the most of the short time we have together. My mind could not shift from Jessie and how she must be feeling. She had explained her sadness at having to leave me before her return. Her mother had not even been there to collect her. That duty fell to Jessie's aunt Becky and Casey's dad.

Becky being there was fortunate as Jessie did indicate that if Becky were not there, then she would refuse to go; part of the reason that I had waited in the car. I did not want drama. Jessie had to return into her mothers care whether we liked it or not. Of course, neither of us liked it, but we had a court order to adhere.

Later that day, I checked my phone for messages. Jessie had sent me a text message displaying her unhappiness at the situation.

Love you miss youuuuu I'm at nannys

(Sad face)

I wished her a goodnight and shared my love. She would be spending the night at the grandparents home. A place she does not feel welcome with people that have an agenda against Jessie and a vendetta against me. Jessie was less than enamoured by this arrangement. We had anticipated that she would return north when her mother collects her; however, her mother did not receive her. It was her family.

As Jessie was travelling on the train north on Sunday, I sent her a text message.

Love you so much. See you soon (hearts)

Jessie's response was swift. She poured her heart onto the page. Well, emoji hearts. They filled the screen preceded by a simple reply.

No I love you so so much

Jessie sent me a short video recording which had only lasted a few seconds in duration. It was clear that she was looking after the belongings alone in her seat. She whispered, "On the train." It was in response to my wondering what she's doing.

I immediately broke down in tears; usually strong and unemotional. Jessie is my weakness. I had spent a week with her. After a short transition, she came out of her shell, back to the real Jessie. The fun, charismatic, charming and playful girl we all know her to be, but in the video, she was pale and reminiscent of her mother. Within just a few seconds, I was disturbed and scared for my beautiful daughter. Such a drastic change in her within 24 hours of being returned into her mothers care. I agreed to hand her over near the grandparents home at lunchtime on Saturday. She had to endure an entire day with them.

Jessie deserves the best in life, surrounded by people that cherish her, and allow her to be herself. No agendas. No mind control. And most importantly not forced to keep her feelings inside. The more I hear from Jessie, and weigh up the seemingly minor comments Connor or Casey makes the bigger picture becomes clear. Connor's outburst to me about Jessie having a mother and Jessie's inability to share her feelings openly with Connor adds up to Casey continues to have breakdowns in her mental health. The court order stated that she should be making me aware as it impacts upon Jessie's welfare. It would not be a cause for me to remove her from her care, but at the least, we would be able to communicate and come up with a solution that eases any negative impact upon Jessie. Without dialogue, there is no way forward.

If Casey is struggling, then I can understand Connor being protective. If she shows symptoms, then he has bared witness for three years. I endured it for eight years, so I do know her much better as she allowed herself to be vulnerable and speak to me openly. I cared deeply about her and did the best I could to support. Connor arrived in her life during a turbulent moment and been there throughout court proceedings. Casey continues upon the lies about being abused. It would mean that Connor has not seen the real Casey. He only gets the parts she decides to show him, and she can be manipulative playing on her illness even when she is okay. It is a minefield of chaos. While there is some sympathy, she also bought it on herself. Connor can place Casey first. That is his prerogative. I, however, will always put Jessie first. She is my only interest. While Casey plays the victim and creates drama, it is Jessie that suffers. She never wanted to move away, yet she is dragged back and forth. Every-time she comes home she wants to stay. Any notion of having time together somewhere else gets knocked back. She wants to go home, and that is that. If it were not for me, who would listen to what Jessie wants? The answer is no-one. Connor and Casey's family will be pandering to Casey and Emma. The only travel Casey does is for Emma. Never for Jessie; just used as a way of getting a cheaper family ticket.

As soon as Jessie arrives in Liverpool, she fails to respond. The only change to her lifestyle is Connor. His control of the family is evident to me, and I am sure to others too even if they have not said anything. For all, I know Casey's family have spoken to her about him, but for obvious reasons, no-one is going to inform me of their opinion. What I do know is that Emma does not sit quietly. She creates mischief and division within relationships. If Connor is half as bad as I think he is, then she would have made her feelings known at the earliest opportunity. They despise each other, Jessie says even more than Emma's dislike of me. She is challenging to get along with and very single-minded. I could not fault Connor for having problems with her, but from what I hear, he does not at least try to get along.

Jessie later told me that Becky only stayed long enough to walk with her to the end of the path. She had spent plenty of time with Emma, but as eager as Jessie was to see her, she wouldn't make time for her. The grandad tried to talk to Jessie, but she wasn't interested in him. In all honesty, she hates him, and I know why because she has told me. The negative remarks about me cause a fire to burn inside of her. She takes it a personal insult to her; such is her protectiveness of me. It's not for me to mend their relationships. The people involved are grown adults, more than capable of remedying the situations if they cared enough to try.

Casey's mother never bothered with Jessie, and she in-turn kept herself to the company of Casey and Emma. She no longer feels comfortable with Casey's side of the family. When one of Casey's sister's boyfriends arrived that bought excitement to Jessie, but it was a fleeting visit which then left her in a place she wished to leave.

34

FAMILY MOMENTS

It's impossible to recall every moment in full detail from the many situations Jessie, and I find ourselves with family members. I have a large family and Jessie is an integral member. All love her. Jessie and David-James get along wonderfully. She is thrilled when he comes along for the journeys with us. David-James has had problems in the past, but time and time again showed that family comes first in his life. Not only with me, but everyone within the family. Whenever they need him, he is there without fail—a true unsung hero.

My uncle Chris has health problems, requiring him to live with an oxygen tank. It's a difficult life for him, but he has always preferred his isolation and his own company to being around others. Overstay your welcome, and he can become agitated. We have visited him at his home and hospital on numerous occasions. For now, he is comfortable back at his home where he often asks my mum for updates on Jessie and looks forward to her visits. When my siblings and I were younger, we never had that from him, but as people age, the little things in life give the most pleasure. In a short space of time, he has witnessed Jessie grow and mature. He loves to see her and Oakley.

On a recent visit with Jessie, I greeted, "Apparently, you've wanted to see Jessie?"

"Yes, I have," Chris answered with a smile.

He then beaconed for Jessie to get his wallet from a draw and proceeded to give her £20 pocket money. A kind gesture which didn't end there. He also had her do an Easter Egg hunt in his wardrobe for her to choose whichever one she wanted. Jessie was a little embarrassed about getting his wallet and receiving money but kept her manners, "Thank you."

It was nice to see Jessie receiving love from family, but I also enjoy the visits. They don't happen often enough, or as frequent as he would like as he is almost homebound and life has a habit of getting busy between visits. He is incredibly funny, more so than I had ever realised. We share the same humour, which sometimes can be at someone else's expense. Later Kerrie, Tilly and my mum arrived. Chris called Mum and Kerrie thick softly to Tilly and I. He wondered how my mum could even be his sister. To the wrong people, possibly misperceived, but although he probably meant it, and I am sure that he did it was said with sarcasm. I'm protective of mum but I found it amusing, as I also poke fun sometimes, okay, maybe often. That's just my humour. I dish it out, but I can take it too. What's life without a bit of banter?

Chris has been fantastic. It's a shame that life took him in a different direction away from family for many years, so much so that Casey probably doesn't even know him, but better late than never. I will cherish these moments, and I hope that Jessie remembers too.

My sister Kerrie has her up and down moments. Ask anyone in the family, and they will say the same. I often take it personally when she alters plans or distances herself, but I shouldn't be quick to judge. I suffer depression now and again, and I know she still struggles with the loss of our step-dad. In psychic readings, he has often mentioned the need to communicate with her as she is struggling to come to terms with the situation. Maybe she suffers more than I realise. I don't like Jessie being pulled in and then pushed away. She's had a fragile life as it is, she doesn't need more confusion and instability, but while Kerrie tries to portray the perfect life, maybe she has her demons to contend. I can be impulsive and not see the signs. When she is open to spending time with the family, it is excellent. We all enjoy her company, and she is a wonderful sister. We have had our issues in the past, but it comes from misunderstandings and not knowing the profound problems within each other's lives.

Kerrie and her husband Lee provided a fantastic Christmas for the second year running. They took on the mantle of being hosts after our step-dad passed away. They couldn't have done more and splashed out to make it a dream day. The most recent Christmas wasn't the same without Jessie but still a great day with many of us in attendance, including

Lee's parents who are lovely and friendly. Oakley missed Jessie; it impacted on his Christmas. He had hoped to see her, and I know Jessie was hurting too. She may have missed Christmas with us, but we returned to visit the day after Boxing Day. The kids had a great time together. We took them to a play centre for the day to run around and burn energy and then went back to Kerrie's so they could continue playing. Oakley and Jessie together are like kindred spirits. These two were born to be best friends, so much so in fact that Jessie has forbidden me ever to relocate as she wants to remain nearby to Oakley.

My adult niece Tilly has teenage twin daughters Celsay and Clarissa along with Elaina, who is a similar age to Jessie. She adores Celsay and Clarissa. We have had many fun days out to the beach, woods and picnics. When Casey and I were a family, the twins often stayed with us during the holidays as Emma enjoyed playing with them. Jessie became close, and they have grown up as great friends. Tilly is a wild care-free lunatic. Picture Rebel Wilson, and you will have her down to a tee. She is incredibly funny. When we are together, it is a riot. Neither of us has much of a filter when it comes to humour, but she goes further than me. Many laughs ensue which Jessie enjoys witnessing and sometimes jumps in to participate. It is a seriously fun household when everyone gets together. Mum often moans at the thought of everyone ascending on her home, but even she can't deny that it is always fun, although maybe a bit loud.

Shelly lives in Norfolk many miles away, around half of the distance to Jessie in Liverpool. The area she lives and the people nearby often bring drama, more than I can bother to witness. It does impact on my decision to visit. As time goes on in life, I move away from drama. It's not worth the agro, although when we do visit, we have fun. At one point, I had the entire neighbourhood of kids with me to take to the park. Their parents couldn't be bothered to accompany them, and I had become fed up watching kids forced to play in the street. It was a challenge as at one point half-were ready to return home while others wanted to remain in the park. I put it up to a vote and made it clear when the majority favour a return back then we leave—resolved that issue.

Jessie and I had some adventures in Norfolk. We bought my nephew Harvey along with us as we traversed through fields to explore the landscape. They enjoyed the freedom to walk areas they had never been before—certainly nothing like the urban metropolis of a city.

On another occasion, we went as a group to Sandringham, the Queen of England's country retreat. It was a beautiful and vast woodland with a play area near the car park. A church was out of view which later in the day Jessie, Harvey and I found. Shelly and her husband Colin weren't interested enough in the Church to go looking. It was a magnificent spectacle. To think that nobles and royalties from the past would've been there for congregations was surreal. Back in the day, we regular folk would never have had access to this location. I don't follow a religion, but I admit to being awe-inspired at the significance of where we were.

Jessie and Harvey both took turns to stand where the bishop would've held his sermons. Jessie understood the significance of where we were. It was great to open to her mind to history and the monarchy. Only a week or so prior the news headlines reported on Prince Phillip crashing nearby not far from the grounds we were visiting.

After, we headed a few miles north of Sandringham to Hunstanton Beach. The tide was out, but the sand was smoother than expected and presented incredible views of the North Sea. I played with Jessie and Harvey in the sand, but then we ventured out further in-line with the tide. It didn't feel comfortable as our feet kept sinking into the wet sand. Other people went further out than us, but I ordered a hastily retreat. I refused to take the risk of us when the tide inevitably comes back in. The kids found a small reservoir half-way back to the beach, which they used to splash and slide. We stayed there for a while before heading back to the beach drenched. By the time we reached Shelly and Colin, sand had stuck to us like glue. We tried our best to shake off us much as we could before heading back to the car and commencing the journey back to Shelly's home. A beautiful family day out.

On another visit, we have had days out in Peterborough at a water park and large country park. Maldon and Southend-on-sea were further fun days out for the family. I don't just keep the moments with Jessie local at home, although she would on instinct prefer to be home. I like to surprise her sometimes, and she has a wonderful time. We can look forward to creating many more memories. Most of which happens during the summer months when we can enjoy the outdoors and make the most of the sunshine.

In between these moments, we regular dine out with family at restaurants, movie nights, takeaways, baking, crafting and many activities. Considering that Jessie is only home for almost a single day after travel every fortnight and a few days in the holidays we do well with our time. It's the life she dreams of having, and I sometimes have to remind her that we are living it now. I know she doesn't like to return north, but she needs to realise that she does come back.

35

CASEY

The bitterness between Casey and I show little sign of abating. If anything it worsens with each day. The love I had for her has turned to unrelenting hate. I don't trust her on any level and feel animosity within her presence. It is like standing next to evil. Her aura drains any positivity. Sadly Casey's behaviour affects me daily with our daughter. I see the suffering she endures and can't help but be concerned. Every word I say gets twisted and used against me. There is no genuine interest in engaging with me regarding the welfare of our daughter — just evidence gathering and provocation to gain a reaction.

To think at one moment in my life I would've married Casey is unthinkable now. She is not the person I had adored, but an impostor pretending to be all that I loved. Casey played me like a fiddle as she does everyone; always the helpless victim. I came to her rescue as the knight in shining armour. Then she twists events into her favour while digging the knife in my back grinning with pleasure as she witnesses me squirm and suffer. That is the real Casey.

I thank God that her grip over me has ended. I have seen the light and through all of her deceptions. With clarity and wisdom, I fight against evil. Fool me once, but never twice.

Casey continues to play the victim card. We have never once since she left sat down and had a meaningful conversation. Instead, there is misunderstandings and accusations. I mean, how can we have a conversation when there are constant accusations levied at me of wrongdoing, and she acts up for attention. We are hardly on the same wavelength. Her mind will be planning ways to betray and twist my words.

For someone that struggles with mental health, you would think that she would prefer a peaceful life rather than animosity, yet she doesn't think for herself. Every response to any communications takes hours or days to be received. It is as though either her boyfriend Connor or her mother have to concoct an answer on her behalf. I respond immediately and stand by my every word. That's the difference. She doesn't know what she's saying from one moment to the next and then gets confused and denies saying anything.

It has been three years since we separated, if we can't get on on just a basic human level within that time, then it will never happen. I have made my peace with that fact. It's not what Jessie would want, and I know that it does sadden her, but I can only do so much on my own. Until the mind-games stop, there can never be a resolution moving forward. It shouldn't be so hard to put our daughter first and make those tentative steps together as a united front guiding Jessie into her teenage years but instead destined to do so without each other's input or cooperation.

I have given up with the diplomatic softly, softly approach. It doesn't get anywhere. I have learnt enough over the years that Casey has no interest in negotiating or taking a genuine interest in someone else's perspective or opinions. Rather than pander to her ego, I inform her of what will be happening — no room for negotiating. I am not stupid enough though to go against the orders of the court. My actions aren't a ruse to upset Casey or to cause a reaction; always done as a genuine need. Nowadays, I type a message in the notes app on my mobile phone. Read it back to myself and give me time to decide whether to send or move on. Casey will react to anything she receives, whether it is good or bad. As I have said countless times, she twists my words and grabs the opportunity with both hands. I know that as soon as I hit the send button, I am going to get an adverse reaction. It's guaranteed. She is predictable.

An example of this is a message I had planned to send to Casey. I wanted to display kindness and let her know that I am here if needed, but after reading, I knew that it would be scrutinised and fall on deaf ears.

For the record I never begrudged you leaving. Everyone has the right to leave a relationship. My issue is how you did it, the ridiculous distance, and the lies. Jessie had said she didn't want to go back and was in tears during our half-term holiday. As I'm an adult I can speak my mind. A child can't. She keeps so much to herself. Jessie told me that she gets sad a lot in Liverpool, even during school. This was hard to hear. I'm not saying it to hurt you but in the hope that you sit and listen to her without judgement and become her best friend or get her that helping hands lady back. At the moment she says she gets on better with Connor even though he has severe mood swings and abrupt. She is so much fun. I wish you, and she got on better. I genuinely just want her to be happy.

I only mention court because she wants to come home. If she decides differently, I won't pursue her return. She has strong opinions which she has formed on her own. To this day she still says "We were only supposed to go to the dentist." A reference to the day she left. I know deep down you care. I wouldn't have wanted to marry you back then if you didn't. Somewhere along the way everything muddles but Jessie needs attention and fewer rules. The PG movies don't help nor does the bedtime routine. I'm just saying to help.

It was a long message to get so much off of my chest and hopefully build a positive relationship going forward. The fighting doesn't get anyone anywhere, but I knew that it would get dismissed and somehow used against me, so I didn't send. Instead, a less diplomatic message was sent which Casey did not like. I had reached the end of my tether throughout the evening and into the following morning. February 2020, the UK faced up to 80MPH strong winds and widespread flooding, which closed airports and train lines. They had travelled home via trains all the way north. At no point was I updated on Jessie's safety or progress upon arrival.

I don't want to hear any complaints about me not texting when arriving home in future, nor should the burden be placed on Jessie. You NEVER update me when she arrives in Liverpool, even when there are severe winds and flooding. I've been worrying whether she travelled okay, but who cares how others feel. Handover locations were only supposed to be temporary. I don't think the judge expected us to be in this situation more than a year on. In future, I will only agree to travel if its' closer to my home and estimated arrival times provided. I didn't know anything all week about her return. I'm not driving all over Chelmsford anymore. As the judge said, Jessie prefers the car journey so I'll just get her if you continue to make it difficult. Holidays aren't difficult; it's the exhausting weekends.

Casey was fuming. She doesn't like being spoken to and having no power. By being assertive, it took her off guard and left her at my mercy for once. She only travels for Emma's benefit. Never for Jessie. If she did it for her, we wouldn't have the problems. She stops twelve miles away on the train to be near her friends home and Emma's dads.

Meanwhile, the journey I drive is thirty minutes in both directions to collect Jessie when Casey could stay on the train and disembark near my home as most parents would do. No longer will I be pandering to her nonsense. It's only fair that as I return Jessie near their home, Casey should be doing the same for me. After all, she only travels a couple of times throughout the year.

In all honesty, Casey drives me crazy. She is selfish, but I think it is only fair to take a moment to reflect and explain what she does well. Casey isn't an insatiable monster who neglects her kids. In-fact she is far from it, she just makes bad decisions and struggles to focus on their needs and desires above her own.

Jessie and Emma are both treated to pocket money, gifts and clothing. They certainly don't go without, and I have never worried about Jessie in that regard. She is more than adequately clothed and now has a lunch box with an array of food offerings for her school lunch. An improvement on the shameful lunch Jessie contended with throughout Court proceedings. Better late than never, and I do applaud her for that. She also prepares improved meals now too, which is a relief as they were heavily reliant on takeaways. Most certainly a step in the right direction. Jessie is allowed friends over to play which gives her a positive social environment. I do worry though that if it weren't for her friend's, life would be more disturbing for her. It is all well and good getting the basics right, but she rarely gets attention from her mother and they hardly ever go out to dine or for entertainment. However, they have had a random excursion to the theatre and a weekend caravan holiday.

When it comes to Jessie, my concerns are mental, not physical. She is appropriately bathed, hair brushed and presentable. Her chaotic life is the issue and the fact that no-one listens to her. She has a voice muted to their ears. Casey and Connor only choose to listen to what they want to hear. Any other time dismissed to her bedroom and a far cry from the lifestyle she has with me.

Jessie has made me aware a few times of Casey's intention to take a driving test, however it never materialises. The reasons for her reluctance are not clear. While I expect her to travel to collect Jessie for her return on Sundays, which irritates me to no end that she doesn't, I wouldn't expect her to drive the journey. Travelling by plane or train would be more practical for her. Driving is an arduous task even for experienced drivers. Five-hundred-miles or even half that is too much for a novice driver. I worried that maybe Casey thought I would expect her to drive the journey if she were to pass so I sent her a message to possibly put her mind at ease.

For the record if you ever take your driving test I wouldn't expect you to meet me half way. Jessie mentioned it a few months ago. It is a dangerous journey, which only experienced drivers should endure. I wouldn't trust many with it, certainly no-one on my side of the family.

The weather conditions change vastly throughout the journey; glaring sun in your eyes, heavy rain and strong winds. Speed restrictions go up and down with accidents and roadworks. Tiredness and concentration are real factors which would push anyone to the edge as you can't lose focus for a moment. The faster you drive the worse it gets. I have no choice but to hug the fast lane as too many mile to get through. I grab energy drinks for the journey home and by then I'm pale and look ill. Jessie's never at risk. I've had a nap twice before I refused to drive when I get too tired.

I'm only saying it as I wouldn't want you worrying that if you pass a test you'd be expected to drive because that wouldn't be the case beyond what you feel is comfortable. I've seen you drive. You would do well on a test. I just wanted to clarify. Certainly wouldn't want that to be a factor in you not taking a test.

36

DEPRESSION

The mind is fragile, often unexplained drops in mood and thought can be prevalent without warning. I would say that I am probably one of the strongest mentally of anyone I know, but even I have limits. The burden of separation from Jessie takes a toll on me, as does life's ever-evolving issues. Finances have a significant bearing on the human psyche. I often feel trapped, unable to transition into the carefree life we all strive to achieve. No-one wants a stressed life, but it is there all the same. How we manage that stress is up to us.

Most days, I am fine. My mindset allows me to navigate through the minefield of chaos without much impact, but then there are *those* days—moments appearing out of nowhere. They creep up and cause crippling episodes of exhaustion and suffering. I guess you could say that I continue to cope through depression. I don't like to say or think that I have depression lingering over me. I'm too strong for that, but it is there all the same whether I accept it or not. Thankfully I can fight it more than most. I am never allowing it to consume me for more than a day and in most cases I beat it within a few hours. I refuse to let it take hold of my life. I give myself inspiration and a will to move forward. I have much to do and accomplish.

I often get the impression that Casey continues to suffer from her issues, and the expectation is that I should be more understanding. I won't deny that she suffers naturally worse than me; however, I cannot fathom that her life could be more disrupted or difficult than mine. Our daughter resides with *her*. She is free to do as and what she wants as she pleases. There are hardly any restrictions on her life. I am the one bound by the travel arrangements which severely hinder any career prospects. Imagine trying to find the perfect job that allows a free long weekend of Friday to Sunday off so that I can travel while also paying well enough to provide a decent quality of life. Exactly, it sounds easy until the search produces very little.

Court concluded eighteen months ago yet their decision has left me shackled and bound hostage to such a difficult and unfair arrangement. I am not free to pursue my dreams without leaving Jessie behind. That certainly will not do. I would rather live in purgatory than give up on my little girl.

Then there is the little lady herself; Jessie lives a life she does not desire, yet she has to endure against her will. She suffers more than me. Jessie has no choice but to see those faces that caused such chaos every day from morning through to night. Listen to their complaints as one by one they feel sorry for themselves - the life they chose, and the one she did not. All the while, no-one stops to think about how she is feeling except her teacher and me. That is the saddest part of all—an innocent girl lost in a world which has taught her that our choices mean nothing.

Neither of us ever have a typical weekend. The week that I don't travel Jessie isn't home with me, and I am not there with her. Both missing each other wishing things were different. Then the weekend that we see each other is spent travelling resulting in an incredible strain on the mind and body. It's exhausting, and because of this, the quality of our time together is impacted. The holidays are the moments when we can truly relax and embrace the tranquillity. Sadly it is also the time when I suffer the most. I get used to her being home. It feels lovely as though she had never left. The life we both dream. Then the moment inevitably arrives when she has to return home. It's gut-wrenching for both of us; she clings to me to stay, and I struggle to contain my sadness. Always takes me days to recover when she leaves. I am never myself, and those around me have learnt to leave me in peace, although mum checks up on me and always a friendly voice to share my feelings. It hurts her when Jessie goes. She's getting older, and these are the moments they should be sharing, not separated continuously. Jessie loves visiting mum and having sleepovers.

One positive in my life if we could even call it that is Casey tried to pass off her debts onto me without me knowing. I found my name attached to hers through a credit check. Incredibly deceitful and cunning. What she doesn't know is that I only found this information while gathering all of my debts while applying for a Debt Relief Order (DRO). In the UK, it is a form of bankruptcy with fewer consequences.

During our relationship debts mounted. I take responsibility for most; they were my fault. I made mistakes by not cancelling TV subscriptions and other various agreements in a satisfactory manner. Casey, however, convinced me to purchase her a brand new iPad and iPhone just a few months before abducting Jessie. She also took them with her—a scrupulous and callous act leaving me to struggle with the repayments.

The insolvency services accepted my application to clear almost £20k of debts. I had to wait twelve-months of a moratorium period for the debts to end. That period has since passed and I am free to move on with my life. A significant chapter resolved. I am not proud of accruing such a vast debt or having to apply for a DRO. The alternative was many more years of uncertainty and stress. Joint debts are now Casey's sole responsibility. Those one's still remain for her, however I am no longer responsible for them. Bittersweet karma. Casey has cost my family a fortune, substantial sums of money to fight through court and travel while she had to pay NOTHING. The joint debts are just a small fraction of what we have had to spend.

It was about time something went my way, although I would rather have the debt if it meant Jessie was home. I would take that deal any day. Money never fazes me, although maybe it should. I do know one thing though; I won't waste this opportunity for a fresh start. Most of those debts were acquired during my early twenties when I had no responsibilities. Times change and the new chapter in my life begins.

37

FRAGILE

A moment arrived in my life. The hell of all hells. A depression that consumed my deepest thoughts. I can shake off mosts bouts of depression. Once I have pinpointed the cause for the low ebbing moment, I can focus my mind on what is needed to improve and banish the mental menace. On this occasion for all of my efforts I couldn't. My mind would cease to work hard enough to fight off the spell to think. The main reason was due to many issues rather than a single force.

Writing *A Heartbroken Daughter* and *A Father's Daughter* has been traumatising. I've spoken to many people who have experienced heartbreaking moments in their lives. They intend to write a book but can't get past the initial pages. The memories are too harrowing, which causes them to suffer yet again. It's for this reason that they stop and put it off indefinitely. I battle my demons head-on and get my story told. Parties that may feel violated should know that reading what I have to say pales in significance to the anguish I experience in writing.

I'm in no rush for that romantic fairytale ending; however, I do look forward to it from time to time which can drain me a little. I am selective when it comes to choosing a partner, and then there is the other issue of finding the one who likes me in return. I notice a few admiring glances from many women but none of whom interest me. I know that my time will come, but the long transition is hard to bear. Add to this the financial woes and hindered career prospects, the outlook becomes less appealing. I want someone to be with me at my best, give them the world they deserve, but at this moment, the moment of a depressed state; all I can muster is nothing. I have nothing to offer. A broken heart from being away from Jessie, but that is all, which moves me onto Jessie. Hearing her low and craving home affects me deeply. She has her fun moments with her mother, but it's few and far between. Never enough to stop Jessie pining to come home. The burden ultimately falls onto me to make her happy.

I don't try to be strong for everyone's sake, well, maybe I do. I don't know. If I do, it's on a subconscious level. I am mentally strong most of the time. I know Jessie being home would ease the anguish. A euphoria and peace would bless our lives. An inner sanctum of calm, but when she gets torn away, it affects me. The issue I have is that while I try to work through this torment and calculate a positive way to move forward, the clock is ticking. I was due to collect Jessie in a few days. An extensive journey draining every part of my body, and again two days after.

I wouldn't be the fun, charismatic and charming father that she looks up to. Well, I may be able to muster the energy long enough to give her the rest of what remains, but those journeys could take it out of me.

I know that Jessie needs me, and I need her, but we need to take care of ourselves to be there consistently. We had a weekend phone call which had been re-arranged at Jessie's request.

"I haven't been feeling well. Depending on how I am later in the week, and the weather, I may not be able to get you for the weekend." I explained.

"What?" Jessie replied sullen and worried.

"I can't travel if I'm not well, and the weather has been so bad with strong winds and flooding. If it's too dangerous, I wouldn't be able to travel."

"It's not flooded up here."

"Maybe not, but there's a lot of the country to drive through which could be flooded."

"Oh."

"The bad news is that if I can't come and get you this weekend, we will have to wait another two weeks as it's mummies birthday the weekend after."

"Oh, no. No. I want to be with you. I don't want to be with mummy on her birthday. I wasn't with you on yours!"

"It would be nice for you to spend it with her, and it would be her weekend, so I can't demand anything."

"No. I want to come home." Jessie demanded.

I had never failed Jessie. I was always travelling, fighting and doing everything for her. She knew that I would, but I was fighting a darker force in my mind that had to be contested. I can fight most things, but this is something else entirely. If she were just down the road, it wouldn't be an issue, but there are many miles to travel and do nothing but think which is the worst thing for me right now.

Jessie's suffering was temporarily eased as she was having a sleepover downstairs later in the living room with Casey including snacks and a movie. Sounds like a good time to me, but the issue has always been consistency. More often than not Casey only does things for herself, so their is often ulterior motives. Could she be having relationship problems with Connor? Could that be the real reason they are sleeping downstairs? Jessie could be an excuse to be away from him, or it may be a genuine gesture of a mother towards her daughter. Never easy to connect all of the dots, but eventually, patterns emerge, and rarely pleasant for Jessie.

Disappointing Jessie weighs on me and compounds the depression further, but I am strong and would do all I can to overcome this before it affects Jessie. As it is, I have already given her a little uncertainty which simply will not do. There's a need to get my mind back on track and focused. If anything can give me the strength and will power to overcome it, then it is Jessie. I struggle with the travel when I am exhausted but on the flip side of that is I want Jessie home. Life is better with her in it, and I know she hopes that I would come and get her, and so I have a dilemma. Would it be so dreadful to miss one contact and give my mind and body a much-needed rest to recharge, or does she need me?

220

What worries me the most at the moment is how my mind could react when I am required to return her? Could it open the flood-gates yet again, setting me back multiple stages of healing? The hurt lingers deep, and the suffering is relentless. We all have our limits, and I'm very in-tune with mine. Of course, if Jessie is enduring similar struggles and requires me to be her saviour, then I will throw myself on the line again and again. Seeing her would heal the wounds that consume our daily lives, but for both of us, the separation is excruciating.

A few days later I had to know what Jessie wanted to do regarding the upcoming weekend. A text message exchange wouldn't suffice in garnering someone's feelings. I sent Casey a text message requesting an impromptu phone call with Jessie.

Would it be okay for me to have a quick phone call with Jessie? It's hard to gauge how she feels. If she's okay this weekend and doesn't fancy travelling I can leave it until next time; otherwise, I'm okay with coming, but I can't tell how she feels in a text.

Casey surprised with a positive response. When our call connected, Jessie wanted me to come and get her. I hadn't expected her to be so adamant and eager, especially as she had just been playing with a friend. I was sure that Jessie would have told her mother of her decision but felt that I should update her in any event.

Thanks for allowing her to speak with me. Jessie said she wants to come home to me this weekend. I'll let you know when I've arrived at school.

Jessie later told me that Casey had been with her when we spoke on the phone. Her eagerness and tone had surprised Casey, "Why did you say it like that?"

An arduous drive ensued as I travelled North against heavy downpours. Rain splashed drenching the windscreen. Similar to driving through a car wash as we passed heavy goods vehicles. Not the most enjoyable drive, though hardly surprising with the British winter weather.

I arrived with David-James to collect Jessie. There was just a couple of minutes to spare before Jessie finishes school. A very close call. Almost felt like a gift from the Gods. I updated Casey of my arrival. She responded that Jessie's mobile phone was in the reception office. She wanted me to receive it after school and suggested that Jessie has £20 spending money to bring with her for the weekend.

On the journey south, we stopped as usual for a much-needed meal and rest. I had much on my mind, which I wanted to address with Casey. We have never had a one on one conversation in the three years since separating. Messages can be misinterpreted, which is frustrating. I tried to keep it concise but felt the need to elaborate and be detailed in my explanations.

I hope going forward we can communicate well for Jessie. It's better when we can agree on things. I'm going to stay out of the way during handovers. Not to be dramatic. I just think you and I are like chalk and cheese. We bring out the worst in each other. The energy between us is just negative, which I think we can both agree. Neither of us wins.

If we do end up back in Court when Jessie is older, it will only be a residency hearing, nothing like last time. They will want to hear from

222

Jessie but like I have always said it's only down to whether Jessie demands it to me. Nothing is guaranteed. I never pressure her. I only tell you this to be open. I see no point in surprising anyone. You taking her shocked me, but I have no intention of shocking you. I do suggest you avoid my next book. I tell MY story, but the contents don't have to be the future. All of us can change for the better.

I'm only saying what I am as I have no doubt you will hear of my next book which has taken 6 months to write. A lot of which was written months ago.

It was nice of Connor to give Jessie pocket money and I hope he can maintain being positive and allow her to open up to him without her feeling judged. I only want Jessie comfortable. I hold no jealousy towards anyone. I know he was just standing up for you as I used to. I don't hold a grudge with him and moving on from animosity with people. It does no good. Hope you have a good weekend. Sorry if any of what I have just said upsets you. It isn't my intention.

I read the message to family members later. The consensus was that the language was excellent. A relief as I do wonder whether I say too much or the wrong thing. She is always ready to make drama which sadly hinders progress. On this occasion, she didn't respond, which is the typical response to something upsetting or annoying. I have no idea how she reacted to receiving the message.

After sending the message and arriving home Jessie updated me on Connor. Inside I wished I had waited in sending the previous message to Casey. I'm hesitant to send multiple messages, especially when it may contradict the previous but every time I try to build bridges I then hear of something damning which derails progress. Connor had

223

been annoying her yet again. There was a situation with Twitter. I know he stalks my profile, but now he was creating a profile of his own. Jessie told me she gave him a nasty look which he noticed. She also explained a situation when he asked her, "Why does your dad support Liverpool when there is a local team?" By all accounts it was said in a demeaning way to point fun at me. The obsession is strange and not lost on Jessie. She hates him talking about me, and he knows it too. He was doing so in the company of his dad.

As we started the journey back north Jessie said, "Mum says 'There are two sides to every story.'"

"That is right, but in our case, there are five sides. Mummy lets everyone else think for her, so she never remembers what she says. In our case, it's five sides to the story. My side, Connor, Nanny, Mummy and anyone else advising her. I remember everything because everything I say comes from me, but she is right. We all see things differently." I explained.

Jessie laughed, she knows I don't like Annie, and neither does she. Jessie always looks at their house with disgust as we drive past, but I have moved on from them. I no longer care to look. It makes her feel content, not being alone in thought. Daddy is right here by her side strong and ready to take on the world. Nothing silences me or makes me afraid when it comes to Jessie.

I sent Casey a text message on the morning of Jessie's return as a last-ditch attempt for everyone on her side to focus on Jessie. Time is running out for them to do right by her; otherwise, she will be the one living with many regrets. I considered sending the message after returning Jessie, however, decided to do so before and stand by what I had to say.

Hi Casey,

Please be delicate with Jessie when she goes back, she was in tears last night. She finds it hard to leave. Connors obsession of me doesn't help. Imagine your mum was with someone else and he constantly speaks about your dad it's going to upset you and anger. Who cares what football team I support? It's silly things. I don't search for him or you but I know he is obsessed with my Twitter so I've made it private for his sanity. An intervention. I never cared about Emma's dad so I don't understand the obsession. Jessie will always be protective of me it's deep inside of her so why poke the bear in her instead of just embracing time together and forgetting about me. It actually borders on abuse by upsetting her for spite. That's not you but him.

I'm the past. I see Jessie once every 2 weeks and a bit of the holidays. Surely I can't be so important that I'm on everyones minds everyday. I'm not saying it to argue or upset but to explain that Jessie shouldn't have to endure talk of me. Talk about me when she's at school if it helps but please not around her. It's just pushing her away from you and I want her to feel loved by all. My goal is not chaos but for Jessie to grow into a confident woman, it's not to rip her away from everyone but right now whatever is happening at home is launching her to me.

If Court was today she would say "Dad" without hesitation and it hurts you because you all know it too which may explain the fascination of me. Buying her things doesn't compare to expressing love. I don't buy her much but she knows I don't judge and she feels comfortable to get her feelings out. That means more to someone than materialistic stuff.

That can only change if you all change your approach with her. Listen to her heart, no judgement and help her heal. Use what she says against her and she will never trust again so it has to be sincere.

Time is running out you've all had 3 years already. Just 2 years left to make her feel settled. Taking her for granted would be a regret. Believe me I know how much you love her. I have never doubted that. So less games of me and focusing on her would be a start in the right direction. The only time I should be anyone's minds is for handovers. I know you'll see it as an attack but it's not. A last attempt to open all of your eyes. I'm not playing games. I could say nothing, wait 2 years and she would come home 100% but I would prefer to say something and try to make her life less chaotic. If it means her opting to stay with you then so be it as I'm not interested in boosting my ego. Please don't respond to me but to Jessie. I won't reply as I'm done arguing with people. I'm only trying to help.

That would be my final attempt to get the focus onto Jessie. I could've gone on to say that Connor has ruined a relationship with the kids by coming on strong too soon. The kids needed time to adjust to life with their mother. His involvement should be gradual, and even then, he had no reason to come in dominant. Jessie and Emma didn't need that from him. A stable base was required not a juggernaut and certainly not a replacement father. A best friend who eventually grows into a role model and step-dad would have formed and felt natural. Connor's problem is that he is hell-bent on trying to replace me. If he hasn't figured it out yet, I'm not going anywhere, and Jessie doesn't want a replacement. If he can become that best friend and step-back just enough for Casey to make the decisions in the kids' lives, then maybe a stable home life could thrive. It is almost laughable that Casey often tries to educate me on kids, while I watch on witnessing a train wreck knowing full well where their mistakes are being made.

I haven't told them that as I shouldn't need to educate them on parenting or raising children. It comes naturally to me as I have experience of children from an early age as an uncle. I appeared in Emma's life as she was about to turn three years old. I wasn't overbearing. She approached me. I was sitting on the sofa when she returned from spending time with her father. She embraced this stranger immediately. Sat next to me and offered a colouring pen to help with colouring. Children must always come first.

Connor wasn't in attendance during the return handover. Jessie was relieved, "Yes, Connor's not there. He must be at work." A damning assessment. Jessie had earlier told me of a text message exchange between her and Casey during a moment of Jessie sitting with Connor on a sofa.

Connor's annoying

Maybe, but he loves you

Sure we'll go with that

What do you mean?

I provided Jessie with my assessment. I don't live with them, but I can gather enough insight from what I hear.

"Connor does love you, and I think he loves you a lot. His problem is me, and he takes that frustration out on you without thinking of how much it hurts you. But he does love you a lot."

Jessie wasn't convinced, but I genuinely mean what I said, and she knew that I only speak from the heart. The trouble is, I think he believes money buys love with Jessie. It's the abrupt dismissals which ruin if for him. Jessie has told me out of all of them at home Connor is the one she gets on the best with, but he is also the one whom she argues the most. My opinion of that is he can't control his authoritative approach and has severe mood swings. Connor is protective of Casey, which is often unnecessary regarding the children. Allow her to be the mother to her kids. If she can't be that parent, then maybe they should return to their natural parents. It's not for Connor to be the guardian in their lives. Jessie has told me that Casey's parents want her to return closer to home. They didn't expect her to move away for so many years, and I'm lead to believe that there are not too fond of Connor.

I know Casey's parents' issues with me - I wasn't working with a career. They hadn't appreciated the support I was providing her and the sacrifices I made to be there when she needed me the most. In my spare time, I was learning and completed an online University course. The support I provided was worth more than any money in the world. I placed her above myself and inspired her to pursue her interests. There was more to our daily life that they will never understand, but what bothers them most is that I won't drift away. They are a contradiction to themselves.

Emma's dad isn't reliable and lets his daughter down, time and time again. They hate him for his nonchalant attitude, yet despise me for being the opposite, placing my daughter above everything else. They want the best of both worlds. Pull me in and out as it pleases, but neither Jessie or I am their play toy. I am sure that they have regrets. One thing is certain, and that is; the bully's now know that they can't boss and control everything to their whim. Some people fight back, so maybe next time they contemplate doing something similar they will stop and think about all of the parties involved rather than themselves. It sure would've been nice to have been included in their thought process from the start. Maybe, just maybe none of us would've found ourselves in this mess.

I leave them all to their chaotic lives while ensuring that Jessie has a stable base with me. The ever-present parent. She knows that I have her best interests at heart. Many people have told me stories of their traumatic childhoods and that Jessie is fortunate that she has me. They would have loved to have had someone like me in their life.

38

SUPPORT

A beautiful community of people on social media ride the many ups and downs with me. My family are just a phone call away, but they have their own lives to live. I am not particularly eager to burden them with my woes and heartache. Bringing people down isn't something I strive for, so I keep a brave face and try to maintain a united front. Most days, I am fine, so it's not as if I struggle often. If I did, I would never be able to muster the energy to fight on for Jessie. I wouldn't be able to travel for our weekends and holidays together. The big BUT is that when I do feel low, it can be debilitating. I become more reclusive, which in turn makes the situation worse as I thrive in social conditions. Jessie goes through similar too, but she doesn't tell people about it, apart from me. She tells me everything, well, nearly everything. Sometimes Jessie doesn't confide in me until a month or two later. I hate that she feels the need to suffer in silence. Of course, I am incredibly defensive, so any wrongdoings towards her and I inevitably react. She knows this, and I try my best to contain my frustrations which have improved as time moves on, but I do still respond when maybe there are times when I should reserve judgement. Listen more and be that ear rather than her warrior. We can all strive to be better. No-one is perfect, myself included.

So, when the chips are down, I vent and share my woes with the world. Social Media is instant, which is probably the worst way to express feelings and opinions. Some posts I slightly regret, but I stand by every word I mutter. I found a writing community on Twitter which opened my eyes to possibilities that I had never dreamt of before. Authors have read my book, which received widespread praise. Validation from other writers is the icing on the cake.

I put my words out there to the world, unsure of how people would respond. I never expected to hear so many positive appraisals. These very same people help pick me up when I am down. They understand the journey that I have been on and strive to lift my spirits when they need lifting. Like-wise I offer as much support as I can. We are there for each other from all walks of life and countries around the world. We share a common goal, and that is to write and tell our stories. I have transcended from the warehouse mule to academic life from those first words written on a page, and I, for one, am proud of my progress. If anything, it is inspiring for Jessie to witness me successful. Show her that dreams can come true, and anything is possible. A glint in her eye and a radiating smile was all I needed to see. I know that she gets it. A star shines within her, and I couldn't be more proud.

I don't involve Jessie with my woes and concerns but some moments are too great not to involve her. Often so many wonderful things are mentioned about her by other people. They notice from all of my comments and posts how amazing she is, and how lucky I am. It is also said the other way around but I prefer that she has the center stage. Jessie is the star and I am her father. I know that she will eclipse anything I achieve. She is destined for greatness. Every room glows so much brighter when she enters. When she sees the words written by others it gives her a nice boost. A perk to her day, raising her spirits and self-esteem. She knows that I think the world of her, to hear of others thinking positively elevates her instantly. Usually I am humble, but when it comes to Jessie I am not. She is more than I deserve, and feel incredibly blessed to call her my daughter. How I got so luck only God knows, but I live every day fighting to make her proud. Jessie never has to impress me. I was impressed from the moment she was born. Maybe one day she will read these words, but then maybe not. She doesn't need to read it on a page as she sees it every day. We have a bond like no other. A kindred spirit.

39

SPIRITUAL

Perfect knowledge of such things cannot be acquired without divine inspiration...

- Nostradamus

It's often difficult to understand or process hardships and heartbreak. Why me? Why us? Jessie and I haven't lived a life deserving of punishment. I am more spiritual than I realised, or maybe an honest assessment would be more spiritual than I cared to accept. I have always held high values in life. Never smoked while all of my siblings smoke or have smoked at some point throughout their lives. I have never felt the urge even in moments when there was peer pressure and almost a ridicule of being the odd one out. I don't live my life requiring validation or to impress others. I know who I am. What I like and don't like. No-one has the right to dictate another's life.

My mind delves deeper into the human psyche than the average person. It's this strive to improve and fulfill my potential, which intrigues and fascinates. I hardly ever sit still in a single moment. Always something to pursue, learn and absorb. The human mind, more significantly, my mind, is something I learn to understand more and more with age. With age comes wisdom, but only if you learn from past mistakes experiences. It is simple to view failures or hardships as a mistake, but the reality is it's an experience to learn and grow. Without those moments to test us we will never understand our true potential. We need those challenges in life to elevate us spiritually.

I am reluctant to appear preachy or overbearing as that is far from the intention. To understand my mindset, requires a certain degree of open-mindedness. I'm not gullible nor easily lead, and I don't expect you to be either. If I am unsure of something's validity, then I refuse to acknowledge. If an idea seems plausible, then I will hang onto it a little longer and see if I can find relevance to validate. Then there are other aspects of spirituality which connect to me immediately and often on many levels in my daily life, psyche and experiences.

It is fair to say that an awakening has blown my mind on a few occasions. The resemblance and accuracy are uncanny. For instance, astrology has been spot on consistently to simply be dismissed as superstitious nonsense. I am an Aquarius and everything on the chart is me including the daily and monthly readings. I don't use the information to change my behaviour to match; however, it does match entirely. How can I dismiss such accuracy as nonsense? It would be easy to say "whatever", but then that would be denying myself knowledge and growth. I want to understand the universe, and my role within it if there is such a notion. We won't know if we don't explore beyond our perceptions and understandings.

Another moment blew my mind - a lady came to me with information on spirituality. She had read *A Father's Daughter*. Congratulated me on a wonderful read and then without prompting sent me waves of information on astrology which was more profound than I am ready for or understand. In her words, "It's there for when you are ready." I later read my annual astrological report. *February/March someone will enter your life to assist in spiritual enlightenment. You crave a more in-depth understanding, and they will support you to understand and grow.* Again this blew my mind, wow. I have had many connections validated in this way for years, not a one-off chance by luck.

I'm a firm believer in fate and destiny. Our life and experiences are pre-destined. The ending pre-defined, which also goes some way to understanding psychics predicting the future. They have a connection to the map of our lives. We do have free-will to some degree which allows us to make our own choices. Those choices will inevitably end up in the same place, but by the end, our experiences along the journey will range from severe to subtle depending on the path we take and lessons learned. I understand that those traumatic and challenging moments in life are a quick-fire way for us to learn fast what we need to move onto the next stage of our spiritual journey. If we don't learn then the moments will repeat in other ways until we can tick it off as a moment learnt and adapted. It's okay if this doesn't seem real. It is merely my beliefs and understanding of my journey in life.

Depression is us processing and coming to terms with a transformation within our lives often from a traumatic event. It's an intense moment which provides an opportunity to reflect on our path and decisions. I for one feel an immense weight lifted and a euphoria of freedom once I have transitioned from a depressive episode. It's as though my soul has made the most of the time to reflect, and used it to improve myself. Strange that it takes an extreme episode to transition but then again it would be naive to expect everything in life to come easy. Often it is the most intense moments which gives us pause for thought and improve our understanding of life.

An example of this in my life is Casey. I supported her for so long, yet she put me through hell. She was the catalyst to make me learn about me. What I want and need to be happy. I now embrace and enjoy the little moments. I am taking writing seriously rather than an after-thought. I tended to pursue difficult challenges rather than hone skills which came naturally. For me, words flow with ease onto a page similar to air blowing in the wind. The traumatic moment revealed my true calling in life, and that is to be a writer. I have made positive changes to my life and elevated an understanding of my true potential upon fighting so hard for my daughter. I found in me incredible willpower and perseverance which had never been tested before at least on such a grand scale. I wasn't upset that Casey chose to leave me. I was upset with myself that I felt more highly of her than she warranted. I am upset about our daughter and the life she has been forced to live. She deserves better. My hate towards Casey has reseeded in-time to pity.

I believe that I was placed into Casey's life when she needed someone strong-minded for support. In the lowest moments of her life, I was her inspiration and voice of wisdom. She found herself, as best she could and began to shine in spells building on progress in various aspects of her life. Her mother's negative influence contributed to our downfall, but I was there for a purpose. Whether Casey learnt anything from our time together is debatable. Our relationship was draining me from the inside out. It reached the point in our lives where we needed to part. There was nothing more that I could give. I needed to flourish, expand and grow while she needed to try and fly on her own.

I pity her and the life she continually repeats. It would seem that I am further along in my spiritual journey than her. I am self-sufficient, embracing my strength within and comfortable in my own skin. Casey relies too heavily upon others with no confidence in herself. While I grow and expand my horizons, flourish and embrace the next fazes of my life, sadly Casey is doomed to continuously repeat the negative cycles of her life as she never seems to learn. Treats people with contempt, feels sorry for herself, blames everyone else with no internal reflection or deviation from the predictable.

I have moved on from her in my life. With wisdom, I have elevated myself to the next chapter which is exciting. I have learnt not to keep negative people within my inner circle for extended periods. I don't want that energy around me. With that understanding, I am enlightened. Of course, there is still much to learn about myself, which only comes from experiences and situations which are often good and bad.

The situation with Jessie and me is hard to bear. It's cruel on many levels. We will both take something from this experience if we accept what happened and look into the deeper meanings. While we suffer, it isn't easy to find the positives, and I expect it takes Jessie a life-time to understand. She will require time to heal and process everything that happened. With time fragments of moments can be analysed and a purpose understood. I don't pretend to be the all-wise and all-knowing. I do however learn and embrace knowledge. I listen to myself more than most. My own intuition and beliefs hold me in good stead even against adversity. I am here to be challenged and grow.

As Jessie has now reached the age of ten-years-old, our time for redemption draws nearer. We don't have long until the next stage in our life commences. In just a short couple of years, we will be well prepared and ready to embrace the positive changes in our lives.

I came close to getting Jessie home the first time against all of the lies and accusations thrown at me. If Casey fails to raise her game and Jessie remains unsettled then next time it will be a home-run in my favour. I will make Jessie's dreams come true. Underestimating me would be anyone's biggest mistake. I hold high values and not easily manipulated. I fight to uphold those values, and for those, I hold dear in my life.

Our journey doesn't end here, and it doesn't stop at the next inevitable Court hearing. Jessie and I have our entire lives to look forward to and embrace new experiences. She will possibly graduate from college/university, get married, have children, or an incredible career. If Jessie dedicated her life to travelling, then that is her decision to make. The life she has and the experiences she embraces will be her path to thrive. I will support her throughout that journey and be the reassuring shoulder to lean on.

40

FINAL THOUGHT

The pattern repeats with the same predictable outcomes as moments blend into one another. I fight on for my daughter — continuing to place her above all else. Be the role-model that she needs me to be. Every day I fight against exhaustion and stress in the pursuit of our happiness.

A Father's Daughter resonated with many people from all walks of life and various countries. The response was passionate and unexpected. I told my story and left the world to judge and decide for themselves. People were able to see through the chaos and lies against me. The reception of *A Father's Daughter* will stay with me forever. I use its success to inspire Jessie. Show her that anything is possible, and not to let our past define us. Our lives are much bigger than a single moment.

There will come a day, and it will not be too far into the future when there will probably be another day in Court. Neither Casey or I looking too fondly upon such a course of action. More stress and animosity. A repetition of the past. Sadly there is no alternative. Casey will not give Jessie what her heart desires, and I refuse to prolong her suffering. In there lies the issues that bound us so tightly, causing a great divide between us. Casey takes it as a personal insult, and defeat if Jessie were to leave, though I do not fight for my ego or malice. My choices and actions are only for Jessie. If she chose to stay with her mother and half-sister, then I would abide by her wishes. Witnessing her happy is my only goal. Bending a knee or fighting on will be Jessie's choice.

All of this would've been avoidable had Casey taken a moment to think of the bigger picture before she chose her destructive path. If she had left Jessie to reside with me when she opted to relocate closer to her new lover, then relations could've blossomed. Holiday's are better suited for Casey compared to a daily burden. She requires time and space to herself. Having the kids on top of her continually is draining. Jessie would have had the home life she craves, and the holidays would have been an adventure rather than a prison sentence.

Sadly it seems that I am the only one that could ever see the bigger picture and notice how the family dynamics would react to all outcomes. Yes, this would benefit me in the initial pursuit to have Jessie home, but it has only ever been about her. Casey would lose a little financial stability with the loss of Jessie's benefits, but life shouldn't come down to money. It is such a sad state of society when people have a monetary value assigned to their life.

There is no doubt in mind of the love Casey has for our daughter. Sadly she doesn't display affection often and demonstrates questionable decision making. I have

241

provided numerous opportunities for her to place our daughter first; unfortunately, each time my words are twisted, and motives questioned. If she took my words as I meant them, then she would notice the sincerity. Jessie is my priority. I place her above all else. Her happiness, wherever it may be, would make me happy. Her sadness weighs heavily on my shoulders.

If Jessie continues to desire a return home to me, then when that time comes, there would be no sympathy from me for the other parties involved. Five-years is ample time to provide Jessie with the life she deserves. If they can't make her happy and settled within that time, then they only have themselves to blame. Jessie and I don't have contact enough for me to be disruptive so it wouldn't be my fault. Sad to think that she may have spent five years of her life somewhere against her will.

Of course, life changes and decisions alter. Jessie may surprise us all and feel that her life is beginning to take shape in this alien world up north. It can only ever be her decision. There would be little point of me going to Court only for Jessie to contradict my application. I feel proud that the day will come when she will have her say, and the noise around her from her parents suddenly silences. It will be her choice alone. Finally, her opinion will mean something rather than a whisper in the wind.

My mindset has always been long term, never short term gains. The separation and distance apart have been cruel, and especially hard on Jessie. I try to maintain her spirits even when life seems impossible to her. We have endured more than a lifetime of emotional trauma; however, it is only temporary. Moments feel like forever, but the reality is that it is just for another year, maybe two or a few more. After, we have the rest of our lives together. Jessie *will* be of an age where her decisions dictate her life. She may be young now and in the eyes of the Court too young. That will not always be the case. I will fight for her again if she needs me. Until then, we will continue to enjoy the little moments. Make memories and not live life in sorrow. Our time together is precious as it is for most parents. We are not the first to endure such hardships and sadly I do not suppose that we will be the last. Family Courts require change. We need to tell our stories for that to happen. It has been some journey, and this has been our story.

41

MENTAL HEALTH

Mental Health is a serious issue affecting many people. Most of us have or will at some point suffer with it throughout our lives. The depression which I encountered is only due to the circumstances surrounding my daughter, and the constant care I had to provide her mother during our relationship. Without those circumstances, I would be fine. In all honesty, I am okay most of the time. The odd suffering moment does happen, but experience has provided me with the best ways to cope. Every case is unique depending on the person. The reasons can be clinical and hereditary. They can also be environmental from our surroundings, stresses and interactions within our daily lives.

I am critical of Casey for everything that she has put Jessie and me through. It is unnecessary. While I can't forgive and certainly won't condone her behaviour, I do need to acknowledge that she does suffer severely with her mental health. Her situation is clinical and will remain with her throughout her life. For that, I do have sympathy and don't wish to add to her burden. Finding a balance is never easy. For all of the compassion I have inside, Jessie comes first. I can't watch on and witness chaos to her life without fighting for her, which may have a detrimental effect on Casey.

The reality is that I don't see Casey every day, in fact, we barely see each other at all. Without first-hand insight, I can't see how vulnerable she is. Maybe if I could, I would choose my words more carefully or go easier on her that day. I react to her messages and disclosures that Jessie reveals to me. I fight back when I feel I need to, but I genuinely hope that it hasn't happened when Casey is at her lowest. I don't prey on the weak or get pleasure from someone's suffering.

I wish that she would put our daughter first and stop the false accusations. Find a sense of inner peace and tranquillity amongst the mayhem and then maybe we can all live in harmony. It is never too late to resolve differences; however, it does take honesty and trust, which would take time.

I have shared our story so that others can learn from our situation. Whatever the outcome in our future I hope that separated families focus solely on their children. Please don't use them as a tool to hurt the other. In the end, no one wins. If you want the best revenge; live well.

MORE BOOKS

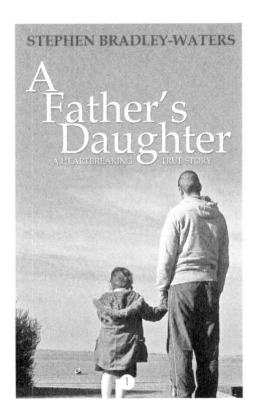

To find out more about Stephen Bradley-Waters visit

stephenbradleywaters.com

FROM THE AUTHOR

Thank you for reading *A Heartbroken Daughter*.

If you enjoyed this book (or even if you didn't) please visit the site where you purchased it and write a brief review. Your feedback is important to me and will help other readers decide whether to read the book too.

Printed in Great Britain
by Amazon